The Chameleon's Underwear
By Gerry Poster
Version 1.1

This page intentionally left blank.

THE CHAMELEON'S UNDERWEAR

FIRST EDITION

By Gerry Poster

A Very Brief Overview of the Principles of Color and Its Impact on Normal Human Psychology

PRESENTED BY THE
DIXIE
LEARNING INSTITUTE

Version 1.1

For more information please make contact with the author:

GERRY POSTER
- DIRECT PHONE/FAX/VOICE MAIL 864-271-4693
- E-MAIL gerryposter@charter.net
- MASLAND EXTENSION 6626
- DIXIE EXTENSION 7915

Cataloguing-in-Publication Data

Poster, Gerbrand III
This book is not available to the general public. The following bibliographic data is provided in Library of Congress format for the convenience of reference librarians desiring to enter the book in their catalogues.

I. The Chameleon's Underwear First Edition/Underwear/A Very Brief Overview of the Principles of Color and its Impact on Normal Human Psychology/
Gerry Poster
124 pp + xiv pp   25.5 cm x 18 cm
"Presented by the Dixie Learning Institute"
Includes appendix
ISBN 0-9724432-2-3

1. Poster, Gerry	2. Color	3. Color Theory
4. Chromodynamics	5. Chromotherapy	6. Applied Psychology
7. Principles of Architecture	8. Principles of Interior Design	
9. Reference		

II. Title

The Chameleon's Underwear First edition, version 1.1, by Gerry Poster, (Gerbrand Poster, III), copyright© 2002. All rights reserved under International and Pan-American Copyright Conventions. No part of this book may be reproduced or utilized in any form or by any means, electronic or mechanical, including photocopying, recording, or by any information storage system now known or to be invented without permission in writing from the publisher. Inquiries should be addressed to the publisher at 102 West Mountain View Avenue, Greenville, South Carolina, 29609-4645.

Manufactured in the United States of America
10   9   8   7   6   5   4   3   2   1

LEARNING INSTITUTE PRESS
PUBLISHERS OF TRAINING MATERIALS

GREENVILLE, SOUTH CAROLINA
MOBILE, ALABAMA
AN IMPRINT OF GPA

To the memory of
Anton Frederik Baarslag (1887-1965),
my grandfather,
who taught me to paint.

"Finally, beloved, whatever is true, whatever is honorable, whatever is just, whatever is pure, whatever is pleasing, whatever is commendable, if there is any excellence and if there is anything worthy of praise, think on these things."
—Paul of Tarsus, in a letter to certain people in the city of Philippi, Macedonia; 4:8 (NRSV)

THE CHAMELEON'S UNDERWEAR
TABLE OF CONTENTS

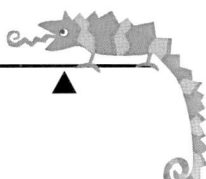

Introduction ix
    Including an explanation for this book's title
Chapter I. **The Basics of Color** 1
    Mixing, Matching and Having Fun
Chapter II. **How Color Works—Practical Elements** 15
    Including why it doesn't work sometimes.
Chapter III. **How Do Dey Do Dat?** 29
    A brief overview of A&D coloring principles
Chapter IV. **Color Trends and Trending** 49
    The wheel in the sky keeps on turning
Chapter V. **A Color Glossary** 65
    7,689 words and no pictures
Chapter VI. **The Psychologies of Color** *87*
    Of Chromodynamics and Chromotherapy
Appendix 111

" 'Yes,' I answered you last night;
'No,' this morning, sir, I say.
Colors seen by candle-light
Will not look the same by day."
   —Elizabeth Barrett Browning,
    "The Lady's Yes"

INTRODUCTION
▲ INCLUDING A FEW WORDS ABOUT THE TITLE ▲

This is a (very) little book about a (very) complex subject—color. Color is an essential component in the way people perceive the world. It has the power to change our moods, attitudes, and comfort levels. It gives life to our emotions, expresses our feelings, and can even embody such feelings as patriotism, love, and confidence. Even people whose color vision is deficient still measure their abilities against those of "normal" eyes, and even those who totally lack true "color" perception see things as shades of grey, which although not colors in the sense the term is used in this book nonetheless are imperfectly perceived *manifestations* of color.

That having been said, it should be noted up front that *all* perceptions of color are to some degree imperfectly perceived. There are three reasons for this:
- First, no two eyes—let alone any two pairs of eyes—see color exactly the same. (To verify that, look at a distant object [or the grey card on page 89] under clear daylight with one of your eyes covered, and then look at the same object under the same light with the other eye covered, and compare your observations. One will be slightly bluer, and the other slightly redder, than the other. Please see below for more information about this claim).
- Second, there are no conditions under which colors can be perceived in exactly the same way, because color is inevitably dependent upon light (which also has color) for its perception (please see the entries for WAVE THEORY [LIGHT AND COLOR] and COLOR TEMPERATURE in the Chapter 5 "Glossary" for more information about that).
- Finally, color is subject to various psychological reactions that subtly but inevitably "color" the responses of the individual to what she or he has seen. These responses are both biomechanical (and therefore more-or-less universal) and conditioned (and therefore more-or-less singular). (Please see the entry for HUE and Chapter 6's discussion of "The Psychologies of Color" for more information.) These complete the cycle of inconsistency that makes all discussions such as the following flawed at best, and dangerous at worst.

In short, color itself is both very complex and very simple. For the Gentle Reader's convenience, the subject is broken into several parts in this book, as follows:

The first chapter deals with the fundamentals of color—what it is, in a practical sense, and how to use it, in an applied sense.

The second chapter is about the way color works, and also discusses (briefly) some of the conditions that can cause it not to work in certain people. It includes a simple demonstration of the first of the psychological applications of color in this book.

The third chapter is terribly audacious. In a few pages, it tries to present an overview of some of the key principles used by architects and designers when they work with various colors in a space—either consciously or intuitively. This is intended to introduce, not comprehensively teach, a complex subject, and therefore is very short.

The fourth chapter also is very short, for a different reason. This deals with trends and patterns in color preferences in the applied worlds of interior fashion and design. Since these trends always are cyclical, and always are changing, this chapter tries to give a sense of *how you can predict trends yourself,* rather than present a mere summary of tends at a particular moment in time.

The fifth chapter is a glossary. It gives you fuller descriptions of many of the words used in this book, and summarizes other discussions, so you can use this as a simple touchstone or reference. Some of these definitions also appear in *Shibboleths and Shorthand* and *The Carpet and Rug Handbook* and are included here for the Gentle Reader's convenience; others refer to more technical approach to color and therefore are unique to this volume. This chapter is a little more detailed than the earlier ones, obviously.

Finally, the last chapter deals with the fascinating subjects of the psychotropic effects of color—the ways it actually affects both normal and abnormal psychology. This is a complex discipline, merely touched upon in this chapter, but references cited in the book enable the reader to pursue the subject in greater detail if desired.

As noted above, some of the information in this book also appears in *The Carpet and Rug Handbook* and *Shibboleths and Shorthand.* They are included here to give a greater sense of the subject of color as a whole; they appear in the other books because this subject is central to the fields of carpet, architecture, and interior design.

And what of the title of *this* little book. A chameleon is, of course, an animal found over most of the world (Eurasian family *chamæleontidæ;* US *Anolis carolinensis*) with the extraordinary ability to change its appearance in response to its immediate situation. This skill—taught for human communicators in *Natural Feelings, Unnatural Acts* and *Intelligent Lemonade*—is a highly specialized version of the protective coloration upon which most creatures, both predator and prey, rely—think the shadow-and-sun striped tiger and the savannah-brown gazelle, or the log-like crocodile and the dun-colored animals that drink at its waterhole.

Beneath the chameleon's amazing adaptive capacity lies many, highly-complicated relationships and understandings—such as, what color is, and how it is manifested, and how it can be expressed. A chameleon does not (indeed, cannot) think about these things, but the human mind can and, in so doing, it can grasp concepts beyond the animal and most other people as well. In this book you can learn how color works, why it works, what you can do with it and what it will do *to* and *for* other people. You can acquire the chameleon's underwear, and with that you can dress yourself for a remarkable journey.

With those thoughts afloat, let's embark on a brief exploration of some aspects of color—because, after all, the fact remains that color is among the most important of the aspects of the visual world with which the reader works. Enjoy the ride!

Gerry Poster

CAVEAT EMPTOR

"*Caveat emptor*" means, "Let the buyer beware." Here, it means that while every effort has been made to ensure the accuracy of this handbook, the author cannot and does not accept responsibility of any kind for the accuracy or completeness thereof on behalf of himself, his agents, or assigns. Final determination of the suitability of the information or material for any use contemplated, or the manner of its use, and whether the intended use infringes on any patent, trademark, copyright, or any other legal protection is the sole responsibility of the user. The assistance of readers in verifying the accuracy or completeness, and in improving subsequent editions, of this book are requested, invited, and accepted with gratitude and recognition; please see the copyright page for addresses.

GRATITUDE AND RESPECT

This book, and the materials that support it, were greatly aided by the generous help of A&D professionals who, while not responsible for anything stupid or erroneous (for which the Present Author stands alone) provided *good* stuff. Many thanks to Mmes. Belva Berndt, Elizabeth Richman Besser, Angela Najarian Collier, Kim Jacobson, Michelle Lebbing, Nancy Ponting, and Melinda Royce, without whom this could not have been completed as it is. Again, *Thank you!*

OTHER RESOURCES: An Annotated Bibliography

Obviously, a book like this stands on the shoulders of countless people and resources, most of whom and which cannot be remembered well enough to be acknowledged or used to guide the Gentle Reader to the wells from which the Present Author drank. However, a few references are available to which you are encouraged to turn for more information about this complex, powerful, and mysterious subject.

And, if you want a "shorthand" version of this bibliography—if you want to know which few books should be at the *beginning* of *your* reading list—the Present Author very respectfully recommends Sherrill Whiten's *Interior Design and Decoration,* Faber Birren's *Color and Human Response,* and John Gilbert's translation of Luigina DeGrandis' *Teoria e uso del colore (Theory and Use of Color),* in that order.

Birren, Faber: *Color, Form and Space,* Reinhold Publishing, New York, 1961. *A pioneering work by a major writer and thinker in the field of color. Out of print; will have to be found used or in a library. The Present Author has seen it on the web in several locations.*
—[Same author]: *Color Psychology and Color Therapy,* University Books, New Hyde Park, New York, 1961. *Like* Form and Space *(note the same publication date), this is a work of imagination and research; unlike it, this book focuses on the psychotropic effects of color.*

—*Color and Human Response,* John Wiley and Sons, New York, 1978; ISBN 0-471-28864-0. *This is the best summation of Birren's work currently available, and brings together many of his ideas as he expressed them toward the end of his career. Well worth reading.*

DeGrandis, Luigina: *Teoria e uso del colore,* Arnoldo Mondadari Editore, Milan, 1984; see Gilbert, John, immediately below

Gilbert, John; translator: *Theory and Use of Color,* Harry N. Abrams, New York, 1986, ISBN 0-8109-2317-3. *A translation of Luigina De Grandis'* Teoria e uso del colore; *an excellent book, with some penetrating insights of great value to the designer.*

Healey, Deryck: *Living with Color,* Rand McNally, Chicago, 1982, ISBN 528-81549-0. *This was written for the homeowner, rather than the professional; therefore, it is a lot more user-friendly than some other books. Unfortunately, however, some of its recommendations obviously are 20 years old.*

Itten, Johannes, *Kunst der Farbe,* Otto Maier Verlag, Ravensburg, Germany, 1973; see van Haagen, Ernst.

Lewis, Philippa, and Gillian Darley, *Dictionary of Ornament,* Pantheon Books, New York, ISBN 0-394-50931-5. *This book isn't about color. However, it is an excellent introduction to the complex world of the designs and motifs used in historical interior decoration, and therefore of value to the budding student of the discipline.*

Mahnke, Frank: *Color, Environment, and Human Response;* John Wiley, New York, 1996, ISBN 0-471-28667-2. *Good, especially in the area of hard research to back up general assertions and claims.*

Russell, Edward W.: *Design for Destiny,* Ballentine Books, New York, 1973; ISBN 0345-2340-27. *An interesting book, "out there" on the edges of mysticism. Well worth tracking down.*

Van Haagen, Ernst; translator: *The Art of Color,* Van Nostrand Reinhold, New York, 1973, ISBN 0-442-24037-6. *A translation of Johannes Itten's masterwork,* Kunst der *Farbe, well worth its hefty $100 price tag—everything one could want to know about the discipline from theoretical and applied levels. The Present Author stands in awe.*

Whiten, Sherrill: *Interior Design and Decoration,* Harper Collins, New York, Fourth Edition 1974, College edition ISBN 0-397-47302-8; Trade Edition ISBN 0-397-47315-X. *This is the* grande dame *of Interior Design texts; it is to its world as* The Joy of Cooking, Audel's Carpenter's and Builder's Library *and* How to Keep Your Volkswagen Alive *are to theirs. If you want a readable, authoritative, comprehensive window into the real world of Interior Design—and want to know the name of a shibboleth that virtually any professional will recognize—shell out the $80 and buy this.*

Wilcox, Michael: *Blue and Yellow Don't Make Green,* 2nd Edition; School of Color Publications, 2001, ISBN 0-9679628-7-0. *An excellent discussion of the specific characteristics of various hues used in mixing colors for painting; primarily for the artist, but great to scan in a bookstore.*

"I'm all in favor of keeping dangerous weapons out of the hands of fools. Let's start with type-writers."

—Frank Lloyd Wright

THE CHAMELEON'S UNDERWEAR

CHAPTER 1
THE BASICS OF COLOR

"Many people would sooner die than think. In fact, they often do."
— Bertrand Russell
Thinking about Thinking, 1975

THE BASICS OF COLOR
▲ MIXING, MATCHING AND HAVING FUN ▲

Color (or, more properly, "hue") is the first thing most people notice when they encounter a physical thing. A car usually is described as a "red sports car," for example, rather than a "sports red car" or a "sports car of red color". The words for color are deeply ingrained in the thought process of language, as well, so phrases such as "a snowy day" or "a steaming jungle" don't need the adjectives "white" or "green" to evoke a picture. The color is already part of the mental image.

At the same time, our experiences with color—and our abilities to express ourselves through the names describing color—are limited by individual experience. The Inuit who lives above the Arctic Circle has several words to describe the various shades of white of snow in different conditions, while the English speaker has only one; the artist has several different names to describe different shades of green (such as chartreuse, celadon and aqua). Thus, we see that color is both a *universal descriptive* of great importance, and a *complicated element* that can be hard to pin down. This book is intended to help you do the pinning. More specifically, it is intended to simultaneously enrich your word-hoard of color-related terms (to improve your ability to pin down specifics of conversation) and enhance the universality of your understanding, so you can apply those terms quickly, broadly, and accurately.

The colors you see are produced by light reflecting from surfaces (or passing through translucent materials, such as tinted glass); chemicals on or in the material absorb all colors except certain ones, which are the color of the materials.

There are, of course, two types of color: *subtractive* colors, such as pigments (paints) and *additive* colors such as lights. Subtractive colors are the ones used in producing *surfaces* that will reflect light (that is, by combining blue and yellow one produces a chemical that will subtract everything but green from the reflected light), while additive colors are used in optics—that is, the *transmission* of colors to optical elements, such as projection TVs or the human or animal eye.

There are three primary colors in each of the systems. A primary color is one that cannot be produced by mixing other colors; it must be produced from a raw or original source. In the *subtractive* system, the primary colors are red, blue, and yellow; they are "subtracted" from the totality of color, which is a more-or-less black. In the *additive* system, white light is separated into a spectrum of green, blue, and red; these, restored, produce white light. Please notice again that *both* systems are important to color theories: your eye uses the *optical* system (with receptors for red, blue and green) to perceive colors made by the *pigments* of red, blue and yellow.

The discussion of color is confusing enough without having to deal with two systems. Therefore, the rest of this little book will deal only with the subtractive or pigment system, since this is the one used for virtually all aspects of architecture and interior design.

Finally, please don't be intimidated by any of the terms used here or elsewhere in this book. They are defined in each chapter with enough specificity for the task at hand, and can be referenced in Chapter 5 of this book as well.

Let's see how these ideas work together in practical reality.

THE THREE PRIMARY COLORS

As we have seen, the three primary pigment colors are red, yellow, and blue. Already things begin to get a little confusing here, because actually there are different versions of the three primary colors used in printing on paper and dyeing substances such as fabric. The primary *dyes* used for fabric typically use simply fairly rich, deep colors as primaries: a crimson for red, a royal blue, and a bright, clear yellow.

Printing, instead, uses a purplish tone called magenta for red, a cold shade of blue called cyan, and a surprisingly weak-kneed yellow as the third. This is true for both commercial printers (as the nice people who produce this book for you) and *computer* printers.

Following are examples of the two sets of primary colors. For the rest of this book, we shall use a sort of "idealized" set of primary colors for this discussion. In other words, the colors used for examples would not produce the exact results shown in this book. That is because this book is intended to teach ideas, not serve as a technical manual. (For more about *that,* see *Blue and Yellow Don't Make Green,* cited in "Other Resources," page xiii.) However, please note that the *printer's* colors shown below are the primaries used for the sample painting on Page 11, so you can see how these colors work in the real world.

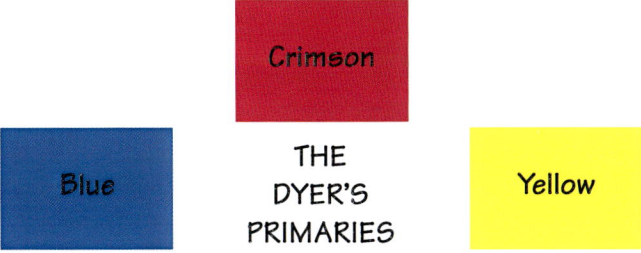

Remember, a primary color is one that cannot be produced by mixing another color—it must be found in chemistry or nature in a "pure" state.

SECONDARY COLORS

The three primary colors can be placed on the points of a triangle, or more usefully on a wheel. This allows showing how mixing any two adjacent *primary* colors can produce *secondary* colors. As we can see here, red and yellow make orange, red and blue make purple, and blue and yellow make green.

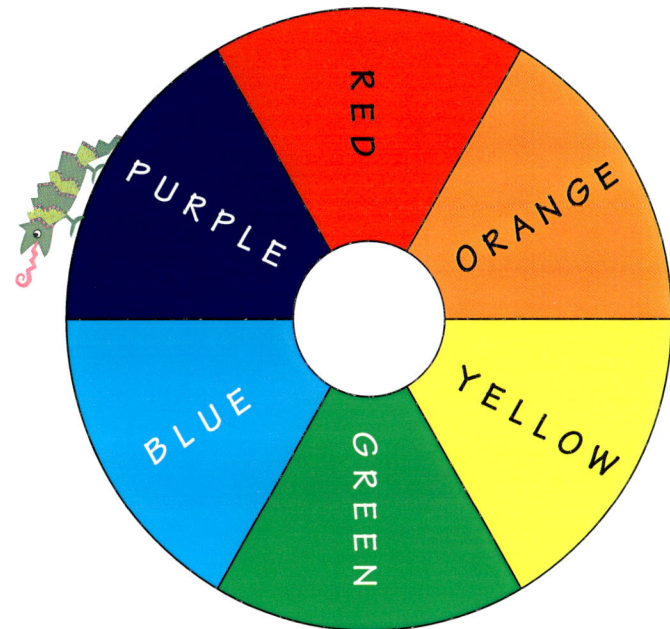

Of course, the colors also can vary in intensity or depth. If the colors are lightened with black, they become deeper; if they are lightened with white they become paler. The most intense version of the color—the "purest," if you will, is said to be *saturated*.

Modifying the relative amounts of the two colors of which they are made can vary the colors. That's why a "wheel" is so useful: it allows showing that the orange closest to red is more like a tangerine shade, and the orange closest to yellow is more of a deep gold. The same is true of all the other colors on the wheel.

Thus, from the three primary colors we can produce all the shades and tints under the rainbow. And when we add combinations of all *three* primaries in varying proportions, it gets even more interesting.

TERTIARY COLORS

From here the discussion splits into four parts: the tertiaries, the concept of saturation, the browns and the relationships of colors to each other—especially the complementaries (which are handled in more detail in Chapter 3.)

Tertiary colors are produced by mixing a primary color and a secondary. They are named by the colors of which they are comprised, as "blue-green," "red-purple," or "yellow-green"; sometimes these colors also have common names (such as "aqua," "grape," and "chartreuse," respectively, but that causes problems—see Chapter 5.)

Here is an example of a color wheel including the tertiaries:

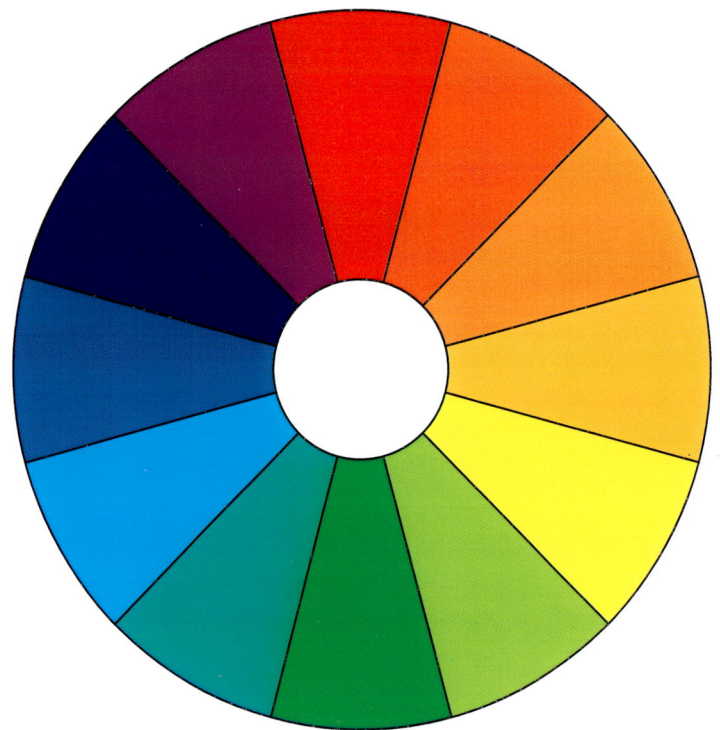

SATURATION, TINTS AND SHADES

It is rare for colors to be found in an intense, pure state in nature or art. Usually, they are lightened or darkened. If a color is lightened (usually by the addition of white) it is softened and weakened; if it is darkened (either by adding black or a complementary—see below) it becomes somber and heavy. If it is pure, it is said to be "saturated."

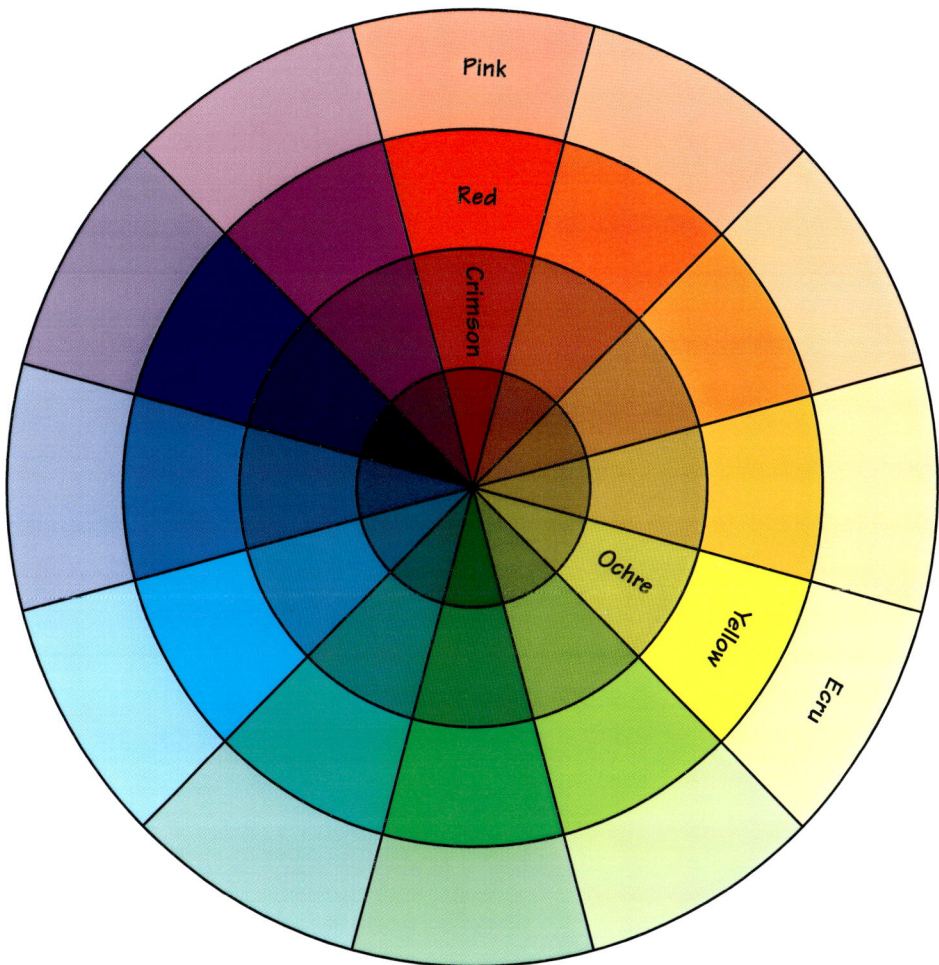

Thus, from the three primary colors one can produce all the shades and tints under the rainbow—especially when one goes to the final step of producing browns.

If you mix all three primaries, you usually get some sort of brown. It should be possible to make black with all three pigments combined equally, but it isn't, simply because no real pigment is truly pure enough to drive down to the heart of Ozzy Osborne. That's just the way it is. Combine any three primaries you can find and instead you'll get a muddy brown; that's why your color printer has four cartridges: cyan, magenta, yellow, and black.

Notice the rich complexity of the colors in the brown family. Since they combine all three primaries, as well as black and white, they literally cover a spectrum of their own.

COMPLEMENTARIES

Complementaries are even more interesting. Any color on the color wheel has an *opposite* color. These are the colors' complementaries—things that look good with them. The easiest trick in decorating is combining such pairs—think Howard Johnson's (blue and orange), Christmas and related holidays (red and green) or about a zillion professional sports organizations (yellow and purple).

Triangular color schemes are also possible. They usually avoid the pure primaries and secondaries, working instead from more oblique perspectives, but the equilateral rule holds true: consider bluish green combined with a reddish purple and a golden-yellow orange. More about that below.

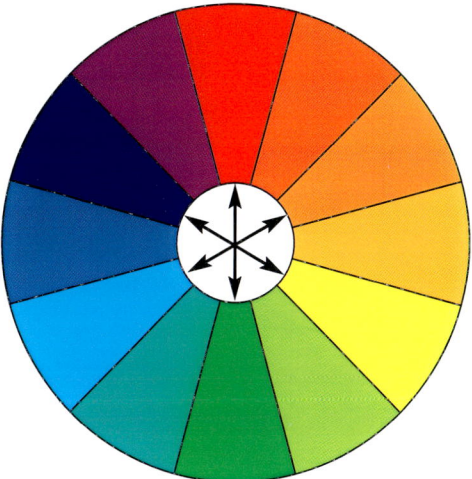

Notice the arrows in the color wheel above, connecting the primary/secondary complementary color pairs: orange with blue, yellow with purple, and red with green, as also shown here:

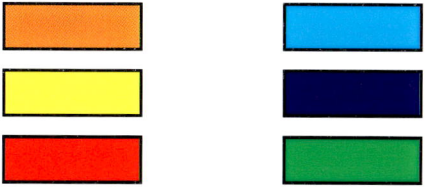

And here are the rest of complementary pairs from the wheel:

DECIDING WHERE TO GO FROM HERE

This little book is merely an introduction and entryway into the world of color. There are literally dozens of excellent resources that can give a comprehensive study, and you may wish to read one or more of them. If you want merely to further what you began here, the rest of this book expands upon the preceding 7 pages, just as the rest of the world of color simply explains the workings of these essential principles. Color is both extraordinarily difficult to master and, as you have seen, quite easy to understand and explain.

What to do next? If you want to know
- How to refer to individual colors with a little more precision, please finish this chapter;
- The mechanical and physical principles that underlie what you have just learned, please read Chapter 2;
- More about how to combine colors and use them in architectural and design applications, please read Chapter 3;
- Something about how and why tastes in color change, and how to predict what interior design changes are likely to be coming, please see Chapter 4;
- What the terms used in the industry mean—along with a general definition of some specific terms—please see Chapter 5, and
- How color's psychotropic (mind-altering) powers work, and what they do, please see Chapter 6.
- No more than you do right now, you're done. Thanks for the visit, and we hope you'll find this chapter useful as a reference. You might also be interested in *Intelligent Lemonade,* by the Present Author, which deals with space, shapes and forms, especially as they apply to human beings, but offers a little information into their mathematical and psychological underpinnings as well.

But as you read on (or even if you decide not to), please remember how very simple the principles of color are. They took only 7 pages to outline, including several pictures. Color is marvelous, magical, and manageable, if you understand the basics.

And as for an example of what you can do with these simple basics, please see the facing page.

Here is an example of the principles described in this chapter. This painting was executed for this book *(by the Present Author, whose brushes and paper should evidently be confiscated)* using only the primaries and white. Notice the wide range of colors possible by mixing the primaries in various ways:

THE HERD—an *hommage* to Paulus Potter (1625-1654)

This is the actual palette used to make the above painting.

Finally, how are we to bring some order to the chaos of naming colors? Since, as we have seen, an infinite range of hues is possible through the mixture of the primaries, and (As is discussed in Chapter 5) the names given to those subtle shades and tints are subject to a great deal of personal interpretations that are themselves colored (heh-heh) by the ability of individual eyes to actually perceive the tones in the first place, how can one achieve any sense of agreement about what a given color name means—what does "red" indicate, for example?

Answering this question obviously requires two things: a constant source of light to illuminate the color samples, swatches, chips, or plates—a source that can be replicated in multiple locations, so they will have access to the same range of frequencies from which to reflect color to the eye—and a comparative reference system that can be placed under those lights.

The first of these requirements is provided by a commercial company. It is called the MacBeth® light, after its manufacturer; it produces a light that is constant, repeatable, and reliable everywhere in the world. If you have to provide a sample, ask to have the original made and the output compared under MacBeth lights.

Failing that, always specify the light source being used—*incandescent* (ideally including the wattage and distance from the source being used), *fluorescent* (including specific color temperature, such as daylight or cool white, distance, and age of the tubes) or *daylight* (including global latitude and season of the year).

As far as the reference source is concerned, there is no consistency in the textiles or home furnishings industries. However, printers—for whom color is a matter of sometimes literally life-and-death consequence—have developed a system, based on the inks using the Pantone® method. These reference points are called PMS [Pantone Matching System) colors and are referred to by numbers. While the numbers loosely tie to saturation or chroma and tint, they ultimately are arbitrary, as any truly useful reference method should be.

On the facing page, please find a more-or-less accurate printout of the PMS system; the "more-or-less" caveat is required because this is a mass-produced book intended for general use. If you wish to go into professional printing, request a PMS book from your vendor. And don't forget to specify the light source under which you will be using it.

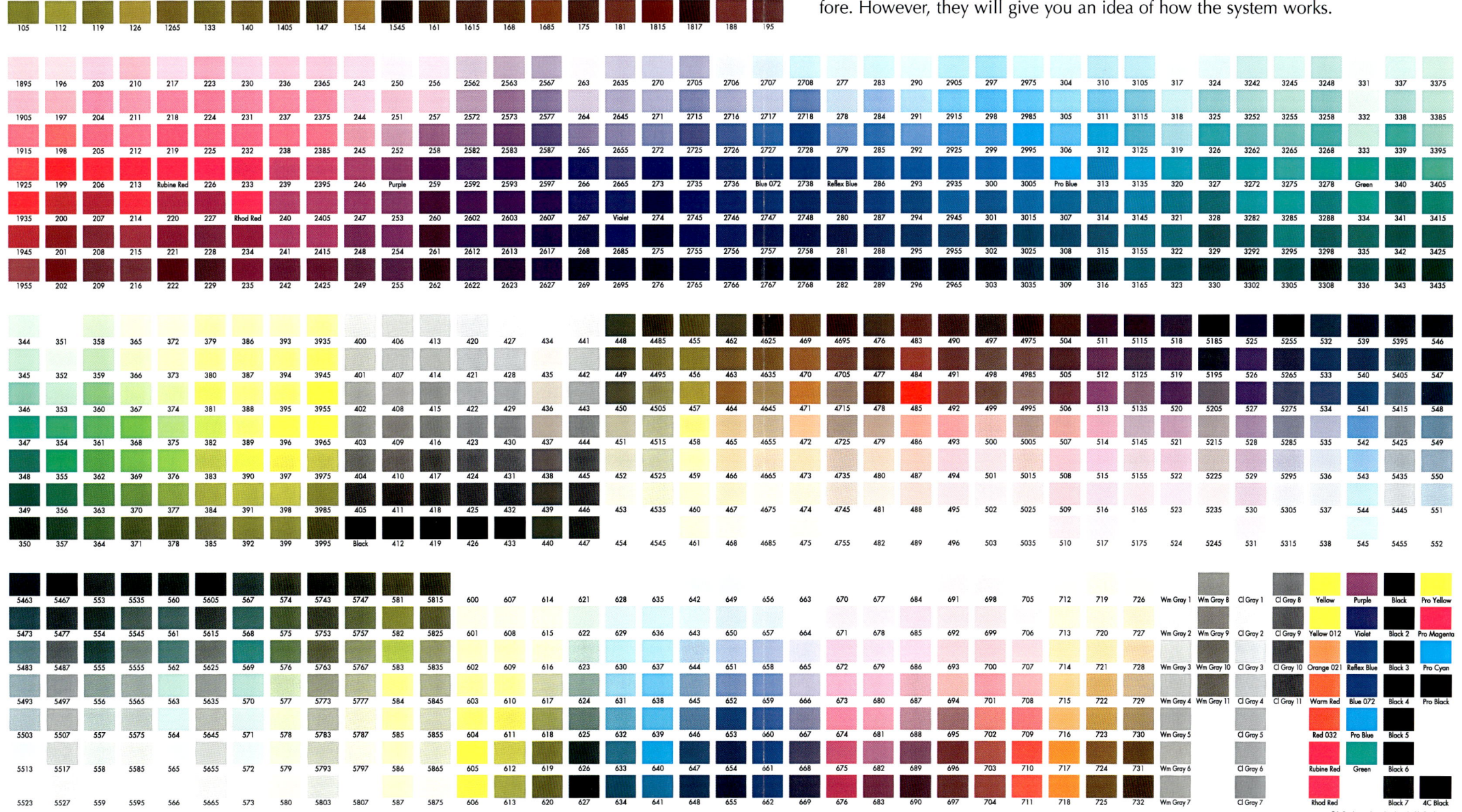

The PANTONE® PMS Color Matching System (Sort of)

As noted in the text, one of the most reliable ways of comparing or matching colors (under standardized light, of course) is the Pantone® Matching System, or PMS. The chips on this page are approximations of the PMS standardized colors--but it is important to remember that true PMS books are printed very carefully under controlled conditions and discarded after a few months to prevent errors due to fading. They also are printed on both glossy and matte (dull) paper, since texture affects color. These were commercially printed, and are not true PMS colors therefore. However, they will give you an idea of how the system works.

For samples of the PMS system . . .

Take a walk on the WILD side.

You might enjoy perusing these. You might also spot a few old friends—colors so identified with a product that they have become as recognizable as trademarks. There's Campbell's 193 red, Kodak's 123 yellow (actually, an approximation; Kodak uses a special yellow specifically not in the PMS system); Masland's 583 green—and Bayer® beige has become so identifiable in this country that even makers of generic drugs use it to identify "aspirin" on the shelf (overseas, Bayer uses green).

"I was going to paint my shutters Forest Blue. Then I discovered the color didn't exist."
—Steve Martin
(spoken by Gaston in
 Picasso at the Lapin Agile)

CHAPTER 2
HOW COLOR WORKS—PRACTICAL ELEMENTS

"Where does the violet tint end and the orange tint begin? Distinctly we see the difference of the colors, but where exactly does the one first blending enter into the other. So with sanity and insanity."

—Herman Melville

How Color Works—Practical Elements
▲ Including Why It Doesn't Work Sometimes ▲

As we saw in Chapter 1, color is an essential component of the visual world. Its simple principles can be applied in complex ways to achieve sophisticated results. In *this* chapter, we will take a more in-depth view of the principles and elements so that you will know how and why color does what it does.

In the process, we will repeat some of the information from Chapter 1 while we expand it, because this Chapter is intended to stand on its own. In other words, if you skipped here because you don't think you need the basics, we will try to prevent a future oversight by repeating a few fundamental points. On the other hand, if you *did* read Chapter 1, this introduction will serve as a reminder of what you learned while it adds useful new knowledge.

First, an important clarification. Up to this point we have been using the word "color" to refer to something which technically more properly should be called "hue." Hue is a graduation or variety of a property by which the appearance of light or an object can be classified as red, green, yellow, or so on. An *object's* hue is determined by the light it *reflects*; it *absorbs* from the light all hues other than its "own." Hence, it is essential for *all* hues to be equally present in the light source if an accurate determination of the *object's* hue is to be made.

Hues are discussed in terms of their position in a light spectrum (plural "spectra"). Each hue has a *wavelength*—an electromagnetic vibration of a particular length measured in millionths of a millimeter (nanometer [nm]). The human eye can see only wavelengths between 380 nm (violet) and 780 nm (red). This defines the limits of the spectrum. In practice there are two types of spectra—one for *light* and the other for *objects*.

The **light spectrum** consists of three *primary hues*. (A primary hue is one that cannot be produced by combining other hues.) They are red, blue, and green. If you combine all three, you produce white light.

The **pigment spectrum** also consists of three primary hues: red, blue, and yellow. If you combine all three, you produce more or less black pigment. The rest of this article deals only with pigment, since it is about reflected color.

There are three *secondary hues* in pigment, obtained by combining primary hues. Red and yellow produce orange, blue and yellow produce green, and blue and red produce purple. If the hues are "ideal" (magenta, cyan, and light cadmium yellow) and mixed evenly, they should produce black. In reality, because of the warmth and coolness of actual pigments, most yellows, reds and blues mixed together produce a brownish grey.

Each of the hues has a *complement*—a hue that goes well with it. The complementary colors are any primary color and the secondary color made up from the other two primaries, and are opposite each other on the color wheel. Thus, red and green, purple and yellow, and orange and blue are complementary.

Complementary hues are very important to designers of fabric colors, painters and other artists, as well as to Architects and Interior Designers (whose uses of the principle are discussed in Chapter 3). If one desires to darken a hue, there are two methods: adding black (which tends to make the color muddy) or adding its *complement,* which actually can make it more interesting and complex. For example, if you study the flesh tones in the works of almost any naturalistic painter you will find that the shadows are painted in tones of blue and green—*complements* of the flesh tones, whatever the skin color being represented. Black or brown would have deadened the painting, while the complementary colors gave it life. The same is true of interior and textile design.

In placing color in surfaces (including fabrics, such as carpets) other factors must be considered. These include the sources of the pigments used to produce the hues, and the method of attaching the hues to the fabric.

Hues are derived from pigments that must bond to another entity's dye sites. The pigments can be *natural* (organic or inorganic) or *synthetic.* Organic dyes are made from animal or plant tissues (such as rose madder or indigo), and inorganic dyes are made from minerals (such as cobalt or zinc). Synthetic pigments derive from the same elementary chemicals as natural ones, but are produced in a lab instead of being derived from the material itself. Since synthetic dyes are much more predictable, consistent, and controllable than natural ones, they are used extensively in industry. This subject is discussed in greater detail under the heading "Dyeing to Meet You" below.

The colors (or hues) used in the process can be understood better if they are arranged in what is called a "color wheel," as described in the previous chapter. A color wheel is a circle showing the relationship of various colors or hues. It has three primary points, equidistant around the rim of the circle, for the primary colors; between them are three points for the secondary colors. The rest of the wheel consists of shades slipping from one hue to the next, making it possible to see the relationship between the colors. Brown sometimes is depicted at the center of the circle, with shades radiating outward to the rim; alternatively, the center can be black or white and the resulting "spokes" can show degrees of chroma, or intensity of color. There is a sample of such a color wheel on page 7.

A CONFUSING CONCEPT: COLOR TEMPERATURE

This is a good time to consider two other words used in discussing color: *warmth* and *coolness.* For an artist or designer, "warmth" is the degree to which a particular color tends toward the reddish position of the color wheel, while coolness is the degree to which that same color tends toward the green or bluish position of the wheel. Both terms, obviously are relative expressions of a color's "temperature," which is in fact a concrete, specific and definable term—but one which has the potential to be very confusing. That is because artists and designers are not the only people who refer to "color temperature": hard scientists do as well, in a contradictory way. This deserves a thorough explanation.

To a *physicist* (as opposed to an artist), color temperature is based on the ability of a theoretical object called a "black body radiator" to emit light by glowing as it is heated to greater and greater temperatures, and the terms "cooler" and "warmer" refer to that object's color as the process of heating continues. For example, as the black body radiator goes from a cool state, at which it is black and emits no glowing, to 900° Kelvin (K) it starts to glow a dull, cherry red; between 1500°K and 2000°K it turns orange; at 3000°K it is yellow-white, and at 5000°K it is bluish-white.

Therefore, you may be thinking two things:
- First, this is very confusing. The higher temperature is producing what are called "cooler" colors. You are right; this is backwards. The terminology is subjective and is stupid. Next question, please?
- Second, you may be thinking that even 900°K is pretty hot. Right again. Next question, please?

Flippancy aside, the reason that so-called "cool" colors are produced by *hotter* objects is that there are two incompatible systems at work here, each of which is trying to articulate the ineffable in its own ways and from its own viewpoint. The difference is of great importance. The physicist or optical engineer needs a reference point for his or her *measurements,* while the artist or designer is looking for touchstones that suit his or her *psychology.*

Thus, the colors white and blue are associated *psychologically* with ice and snow, while the colors red and orange are associated with fire. These associations are deeply rooted in human experience, and shape reactions to concrete experience; for more information, please see Chapter 6 and its discussion of the psychology of color. There also is a much more comprehensive discussion of color temperature (including information about using color temperature in photography, for those people who still admire the flexibility of film) in the Glossary in Chapter 5, to which you are very respectfully invited.

AN EYE FOR AN EYE

But now to another question: what is the mechanism by which the eye (specifically the human eye, since it appears to be dissimilar from the eyes of other creatures, saving only the great apes) perceives color? This requires answers to three encapsulated questions: first, how does color get to the eye? Second, what does the eye do when it gets there? And, third, what happen in eyes where things don't go as expected?

Good questions—and easier to answer than the last two. Let's start with the issue of what light and color are.

Light is not fully understood; whenever someone claims to have mastered its theory, it does something unexpected and the experts clear their throats, shuffle their feet, and change the subject. Although most people would agree that light is fundamentally an electromagnetic radiation or vibration to which eyes can react, it also
- as Einstein predicted appears to act as if it had (or at least is affected by) mass, so celestial objects can bend it;
- sometimes acts like particles (called photons), sometimes acts like *quanta* (packets of energy), and at other times it acts like a wave, and
- is distinguishable from "invisible" energy, such as *ultra* (that is, "higher than") *violet,* and *infra* (that is, "lower than") *red* only in that it has different frequencies of vibration.

Light travels from its source in all directions simultaneously, at a speed currently measured at 186,282 miles per second or 299,972 kilometers per second (although each newer, more-precise measurement reveals a slightly slower speed than the one before, suggesting that it may be slowing). White light is made up of a range of hues, or colors, each of which has its own frequency of vibration, or "wavelength"; the colors are not absolutes, but *shades* on a continuous range.

There are certain "reference points" whose wavelengths can be measured, which humans perceive in terms of response by individual receptors in the eye that sense each of the primary colors (remember, there are different primaries for pigment and light; the *eye* has receptors for blue, green, and red [the *optical* primaries] to respond to the *pigments* of blue, yellow, and red [the primary colors in pigment]). The normal human eye's color receptors peak at 480 nm (cyan—a deep blue), 540 nm (green) and 600 nm (orangish-red). All receptors are quite sensitive around 570 nm which produces the perception of yellow (and are perceptive at some level to *all* the stimulating pigments).

There is more about this business of color frequencies below. And, the foregoing having been said, it becomes obvious here (as it was in

Chapter 1) that naming colors is a matter of gradation, rather than absolute identification. In fact, in *The Carpet and Rug Handbook* the author records an experiment some years ago in which an arrangement of color names—from purple to crimson—was attempted with what can only be called a crashing lack of success. Undeterred, however, he has tried again in this volume; please see The Verbal Spectrum™ in Chapter 5, below.

THE BRAIN DRAIN

So—now, we've gotten the light from a source, to the object, where it has been reflected to your eye. What happens next?

Let's start by admitting that human vision—especially human *color* vision, and even more especially human *stereo* color vision—is not fully understood at this time. What is known is this: when you see something, your eye transmits light through a marvelously designed lens in the front of your eye. Muscles around the lens focus it so that the image is as sharp as possible, reverse it, and project the picture on the back of your eyeball. If your eye focuses well on distant things but poorly on close things it is said to be *hyperopic* (from the Greek "hyper"="far"); if your eye focuses well on close things but poorly on distant things it is said to be *myopic* (from the Greek *myops,* "near-sighted", literally, "blinking"); if your eye has aged to the point where it no longer works as well as it did when you were younger you are *presbyopic* ("old-eyed"). Happy birthday.

It is in explaining precisely what happens after the image projected by your lens hits the *retina*—the light-sensitive surface on the back of your eyeball—that scientists and physicians begin to argue amongst themselves and behave in most unscientific ways. As noted above, there are specialized receptors, called "rods" (sensitive to low intensities of light) and "cones" (sensitive to color and higher intensities of light) [named for their shapes] on the retina; these respond to the light and convert it into electrical energy. This energy is transmitted through the optic nerves to the brain, where it becomes information and is processed into knowledge. Ultimately, it reaches the visual cortex of the brain; from there it is processed and you do something with what you have seen. But no one at this point claims to fully understand how all this takes place, or what processes are involved in the physical interactions.

One of the mysteries is the *afterimage*—a visual phenomenon in which an image persists—in reversed tones—after the source has been removed, as when someone gazes intently at a drawing for some time, shifts her or his eyes to a white surface, and sees the original picture in reversed (complementary) colors on the new plane. The afterimage is due to overstimulation of the visual apparati during the period of intense study. This is important in critical work areas: for example, surgeons in an operating room see afterimages of blood and gore when they shift their eyes, unless the room's decor anticipates and accommodates the problem. (For an example of this process at work, please see the facing page.)

COLOR VISION PROBLEMS

Describing what happens when the process of processing color doesn't work as it should is a little easier than describing the processing of color as a whole. This deficiency is called *color blindness,* which is the condition of having restricted, or no, ability to perceive color, to a degree greater than the normal variations between individuals.

Achromatopsia is the condition of being totally unable to distinguish colors, seeing things only in shades of grey; this is what *commonly* is called "color blindness." As noted above, the eye can see colors because of the presence in the eye of receptors called "cones" and "rods"; in the condition of achromatopsia, there are blocks or deficiencies in these receptors.

If the receptors are only partly deficient, the result is called *anomalous trichromatism,* a difficulty in distinguishing between colors that appear very different to most people. The most common "color blindness" is properly called *daltonism.* In the daltonic eye, cones that should be sensitive to a particular primary hue (a color which cannot be made by mixing two other colors) are, in fact sensitive to its *complementary* (that color which is "opposite" it on the color wheel, composed of the *mixture* of two adjacent primary colors).

Remember, there are two color systems: pigment, in which the primary colors are red, yellow, and blue, and the *optical* system, in which they are red, green, and blue-violet. The eye *perceives* colors produced by reflections from pigment in *optical* system receptors.

Thus, in the eye suffering from anomalous trichromatism, there will be various deficiencies. If the eye is insensitive to or lacks the red receptor, it is said to be *protanopic;* if the problem lies with the green receptor the eye is *deuteranopic,* and if the blue-violet receptor is deficient the eye is said to be *tritanopic.*

DYEING TO MEET YOU

Next on the menu is understanding how all this fits into the world of the Interior Design, Architectural, or carpet specialist. The world of coloring surfaces depends upon two key words: *dyes* and *pigments.*

The two are inextricably entwined. A *dye* is a substance containing *pigments,* words that so far we have been using loosely, interchangeably, and over-simply. More precisely, a pigment is a hue-bearing particle that

Test the principle of afterimage for yourself. Stare directly at this figure for at least 30 seconds, then immediately look at the blank area below. You should see a grey image of the same figure in the blank area—an afterimage. Incidentally—and interestingly—this doesn't not work well for people who suffer from anomalous trichromatism.

will not dissolve in a liquid, but which can be carried by the liquid in a solution. The solution is called a "dye". When the dyeing liquid (often called a "dye liquor" in many industries) is presented to another surface—such as a fiber—in which there is available a suitable dye site, the particle of pigment will leave the carrying liquid, bond to the dye site, and thereby impart to it the hue which it displays.

Pigment particles can be differentiated by size and/or electrical conductivity as well as hue; if pigments of differing *hues* which also differ in their *size* or *electrical charge*, are placed in suspension in a given liquid, and a fabric in which fibers of *correspondingly* different dye sites have been tufted (or woven) is then immersed in the liquid, a *multi*-hued effect can be produced by a *single* dyeing.

Thus, we see that a "dye" is a substance containing pigments. Again, we have been oversimplifying these terms; more information is needed now. There are several sources for carpet dyes:
- **Natural**—vegetable or mineral. These are the original dyes, used for centuries; they tend to fade and are inconsistent in color.
- **Aniline**—derived from coal tar or other sources of nitrobenzene; these dyes tend to be corrosive and unstable, and after their popularization around 1865 fell out of favor.
- **Acid**—derived from acidic groups, such as the sulfo group, used chiefly for silk and wool, tending to be cheap and liable to crock and bleed—see below in this chapter for more information about these terms, or check them out in Chapter 5.
- **Chrome**—derived from the dichromate of elements such as potassium or sodium, these relatively modern dyes are fast and stable.

And where does all this lead? If the purpose of specifying color is achieving a specific design end, the end must be understood as part of a whole. That means that the colors must be matched, and that leads to another subject—the way in which the matching process takes place.

First, a definition or three. Color matching is the process of comparing hues and tones used in manufacturing (or developing an end product), in order to conform to requirements and standards. There are three critical elements in color matching: the *light under which the colors are compared* and the *surface luster* and *texture* of the objects being matched.

ONCE OVER LIGHTLY

As noted above, a perfect, pure white light contains all of the colors in the rainbow, and an object placed under it absorbs all but its "own" color. Objects literally take their color from the light under which they are viewed. If a color is missing from the light, or present to a too high or low degree, the object will not be able to reflect its "own" color correctly, since the color the object *reflects* is what you see. For example, under the yellowish light of incandescent light bulbs, everything will look yellowish, because primarily yellow is available to be reflected. Under cool white fluorescent tubes, everything looks bluish. Under daylight, everything looks brighter. Therefore, it is imperative to state under which light source an object will be color **matched**. One common industry standard is the MacBeth® light (A trade name for a standard light source under which objects can be viewed for color matching). See also Ott Light® (a special bulb designed by Dr. John Nash Ott using rare earth phosphors to produce artificial light that accurately reproduces daylight. This allows much more accurate evaluation of how given hues will appear in use. This is not the same as a MacBeth light, which produces an industry *standard*—rather, the purpose of an Ott Light is to make things *naturally attractive*).

The surface texture of an object also greatly affects its apparent color. A rough surface reflects light in more angles than a smooth one. In fabric or other products used for interiors or exterior surfaces, this effect means that cut pile carpet, for example, will always appear darker than loop pile carpet made of the same yarn—again, because the light is absorbed and reflected differently. (This results in the phenomenon called *shading*.)

In the same way, the luster of the materials from which an object is made (such as the yarn in a textile) will affect the apparent color; higher luster materials (such as fibers) will look lighter than other, lower luster materials. But deepening the dye will still not produce an acceptable match, because is is not truly a *color* matching problem in such a case, but rather *luster* matching—which must be dealt with on its own terms.

Of course, there is more than color, texture, and luster affecting the visual appearance of perceived objects. Among the other factors influencing what you see are the actual construction of the product, and the effects that has upon its *overall* texture. In carpets, construction is generally grouped into four main categories: cut pile (including shag, saxony, and plush), loop pile, cut and loop pile (also called sculptured) and textured loop pile. (The term "texture" usually does *not* refer to the "feel" of the carpet, which is called hand.)

And there's more: things such as the proportion or relationship of the various objects influence the appearance. A primary component here is a principle called the *Golden Rectangle,* or *Golden Section*—a proportion used in all aspects of design. Discovered by the ancients, it can be computed by dividing a line so that the ratio of the whole to the larger part is the same as the ratio of the larger part to the smaller. An easier but much less scientific and less accurate way is to take a rectangle, draw a diagonal, and then take a perpendicular to the line to either of the other corners. Repeating the process will produce points which, if connected, will result in a smaller rectangle inside the larger one—in roughly the Golden Proportions. The psychological impact of the patterns formed by the textures in the construction will subliminally affect the perception of the color—in other words, two patterns made of identical yarns dyed identical colors may still not appear to match because the proportions of one are more pleasing to the eye than those of the other.

And, that having been said, let us not lose sight of the purpose of the present text, which is the application of color to textiles. Within this frame of reference, one penultimate concern must be the *loss* of color, once lovingly applied to the materials. There are several ways in which this can happen, such as *crocking* (the rubbing-off of dyes from fibers under various circumstances) or *bleaching* (the loss of color under the application of [usually oxidizing] chemicals). Chief among these problems is *fading,* which is the loss of color under what appear to be benign conditions—such as leaving the fabrics lying about unbothered in the home. Fading is measured with *American Fade Units* (AFU), which is the standard used for measuring a product's resistance to losing color.

Preventing this problem is a priority for manufacturers, of course. One method of anticipating it is the *fading test,* which is used to predict the likelihood of carpet losing its hue under actual use conditions. Fading is usually caused either by ultraviolet light or exposure to ozone gas; the first is commonly found in any extremely sunny area, and the second in the presence of electrical storms or swamp gasses. *Free* ozone in the lower atmosphere is *increasing* at the same time as the ozone *layer* in the upper atmosphere (which protects the earth from ultraviolet radiation) is *deteriorating,* making attention to fade resistance ever more important. Materials are tested in special chambers, considering the specific hue chosen for an application, the fiber on which it is to be applied, and the construction itself.

You may encounter ultraviolet light and another relative—Xenon—in other circumstances. Remember, ultraviolet light is an extremely high frequency of light (beyond the reach of normal human sensitivity). It is used to call attention to things normally invisible; certain defects—such as slubs and contamination—become readily visible under UV. It is also used as a tool for accelerating the decay of dyestuffs to predict reliability and color stability in actual use. Xenon, on the other hand, is a gas used in a special bulb to produce an intense light by which carpet is tested for resistance to fading. Here, it is the "bleaching" effect of the light that causes the fading.

Finally, we have the issues of psychological responses to the visual phenomena described above. This subject is the province of Chapter 6, below; however, as you contemplate going there, there are three concepts to outline: *chromodynamics and chromotherapy, bioplasmic energy,* and *brainwashing.* These are important but poorly-understood areas in which the *application* of color upon human *psychology* is being explored. Just for the record, then; just as a way of achieving closure in this chapter—*brainwashing* is the replacement of an individual's own personal value systems and beliefs with those of others. The process is associated with totalitarian regimes, and usually is accomplished by sensory deprivation, the application of drugs, psychological stress techniques, or torture. Design, architecture, and the absence of color often are components of the mix; monotony is a powerful tool for erasing thought.

In the same vein, *chromodynamics and chromotherapy* are the study of the influence of color (more precisely, hue) on individuals. Color has a powerful influence on mental state, so the impact of the color in establishing a "tone" or "mood" on the environment should be considered. Again, this is discussed in detail in Chapter 6; in the simplest form of this study, basic *colors* evoke basic *emotions:* red is exciting, green is restful, blue is cheerful (paradoxically), yellow stimulates action, caution, or thought, pink is pacifying and so on. Research shows certain larger recommendations: *workplaces* work best with a complementary scheme of yellow, orange, or orange-yellow with pale blue or green; *concentrated mental activity* seems to work best in an environment of soft and moderately contrasted hues; *homes* should use various colors suitable for the rooms' activities; *stores* can stimulate sales with yellow tones, and a particular shade of pink (called Baker/Miller) is used in *police drunk tanks* and is named for two local problem drinkers who quickly fell asleep the first time they were sent there.

Finally, *bioplasmic energy* is the condition of living (*"bio"*) forms of a highly ionized gas (*"plasma"*) emanating from a (usually understood to be human) body. This is thought to be the source of *auras,* glowing "haloes" perceived by some people around the heads (and bodies) of other people; bioplasmic energy is claimed to be the source. This is an "out there" area although most of the specialists in the field—such as Dr. Shafica Karagulla of Edinburgh and Dr. John Perrakos of New York—are both recognized physicians and adherents of "alternative" thought.

And if that doesn't scare you, the Present Author has only the utmost respect for the Gentle Reader—as he does, in any case, regardless of the immediate reaction. And from this, then, forward—(skip two beats)—into the past. *

---

* The reference is to a skit by the magnificent neo-radio troupe *Firesign Theatre,* to which the Present Author most enthusiastically urges the Gentle Reader.

"If ignorance were bliss, more people would be happy."

—Gerry Poster,
after Philip Howard

CHAPTER 3

How Do Dey Do Dat?

"And Life is color and warmth and light
And a striving evermore for these;
And (s)he is dead, who will not fight;
And who dies fighting has increase."
—Julian Grenfell (alt)

How Do Dey Do Dat?
▲ A Brief Overview of A&D Coloring Principles ▲

An interior designer or architect goes to school and practices for many years to learn the complexities, intricacies and subtleties of his or her art and craft. Most people who tackle this sort of work agree that it is far, far harder than it looks, which is one reason that so few people who labor in these vineyards ever make much wine.

Only a fool would try to summarize the key principles under which this work is done. And, as you probably have guessed by now, the Present Author is just the sort of fool as would rush in where sensible angels fear to tread, and describe some of the underlying principles that the Architect and Interior Designer use when assembling a color palette for a particular project, space, or building.

Color is, of course, the starting point for most interior design, and is important to exterior planning as well. In producing this book, the Present Author conducted numerous interviews with Architects and Designers to discover the sequence with which they approach a project. Both groups (especially those who dealt with a finished space—the Designers) reported that they started by considering the project's desired outcome and the constraints imposed upon the project by the environment, the owner's preferences, and the space's function. Then the first tool upon which they decided when planning the response to the constraints and expectations was color. Thus, we can say that the first step followed in establishing the physical appearance of a space must be deciding on a color *scheme,* and the second deciding on a color *plan.*

The process of employing or using color in an architectural or interior design environment must also be understood as two things it is *not.* Specifically, it is

- **Not** "placing" a color *in* or *on* a surface. The color must be part of a total scheme, integrated into the structure's functions, intent, and design concept. Color also is

- **Not** the only thing that matters. Granted, color is the most obvious thing about an object or a space; often, in practical terms, it is the starting point—the "foundation"—for the design. But it is one of several elements actually employed in forming the space; others include shape, placement of shapes, textures, and patterns. Think of color as *primus inter pares*—the "first among equals"—as you think about its application to an interior or exterior.

Finally, a starting word about exteriors. As noted in *Shibboleths and Shorthand,* one of the defining characteristics of the 20th Century

Modern or International architectural style was the elimination of decoration and ornamentation in any form. For many architects, color was perceived as a type of decoration, and therefore was rejected. Brutalistic architecture and interiors, for example, used the natural grey of concrete; another clear example of this is the "Whites"—New York architects who specifically made their buildings as white in reality as had been the cardboard *maquettes* (models) they had built in their *ateliers* (studios). This was a conscious following of people such as Mies van de Rohe and Le Corbusier.

At the present time, with Modernism apparently dead and an inchoate repudiation called Postmodernism developing, architects are returning to coloring the exteriors of buildings as part of their decoration, at the same time as Interior Decorators are using ever-more color on the buildings' interiors (from which its banishment was both less severe and less enduring than from the exteriors). So the observations made in this section apply to both the inside and outside lives of structure. The photos on the facing page are examples of these trends in the use of color in exterior design; the time represented between the construction of these two buildings is about 30 years, but the philosophical separation gigantic.

Now let's go on to consider what color does, how it does it, and how Architects and Designers put it through its paces.

THE IMPORTANCE OF COLOR TO SPATIAL FACTORS

The way shapes relate to each other in space—the ratio of large to small, shape to shape, and *positive space* [things that are present] to *negative space* [the empty areas between things that are present] are, as noted above, very important to the Interior Designer and (especially for the Modernist) architect. Indeed, while color is the thing first noted about the appearance of a space, the second almost always is the things within and defining it—as the character Sagot, an art dealer in Steve Martin's play *Picasso at the Lapin Agile* says, the frame (the spatial borders) is the most important defining characteristic of a picture. These subjects relate to color only to the degree that color can be used to affect the *apparent* relationship between objects. Therefore, only those psychological aspects of the use of color in *altering the perceptions* of space are handled in this book.

There is a little more about this—especially as these relationships are based on hard-wired perceptions of beauty and attractiveness—in *Intelligent Lemonade,* but even there the handling is light. If this is an area important to the Gentle Reader, the Present Author recommends a good course in architecture, sculpture or interior design. Beyond this—an appreciation rather than a treatment of the core principles of shape and space—we cannot go here.

Above, a typical "colorless" Modernist (International) Style office building; below, an example of the color being used on a representative Postmodern structure, in this case near Celebration, Florida.

FIRST CAUSES

As we know, there are three principle colors (more properly, *hues*) called *primary*; the colors made by mixing primary colors are *secondary*, and color made by mixing a primary and a secondary is called a *tertiary*.

And, as we have also seen, these color names always are oversimplified, because there are several different types or hues of a color such as "red" (magenta, crimson, scarlet), "blue" (cyan, navy, cobalt), and so on. Thus, even in discussing primaries there are variations, and the secondaries and tertiaries are further varied as a consequence.

Finally, colors can be made *richer* or purer (increasing their *saturation* or *chroma*), *darker* and duller (by adding black), or *lighter* (by adding white). Combining complementary colors—the hues directly across on the color wheel—can also darken colors. Variations from the pure color are called its *values, tints* or *shades.*

For the designer, that means that there are essentially three color tools with which to work:

- The **hue** or color(s) of the object and the color's own characteristics (such as warmth or coolness);

- The **value, tint or shade** of the individual hue(s) selected and *their* characteristics, and

- The **relationship** of each color to other colors in the space, and any psychological reactions to those *relationships.*

The selection of the first two tools is determined by the designer's understanding of the space and its function. This psychological consideration is discussed in Chapter 6 of this book; here, let's simply acknowledge the principle. For examples,
- If the designer were establishing a space for a lawyer's office she or he probably would select a color connoting reliability (such as a saturated blue);
- For a topless night club s/he would select a color suggesting excitement and sensuality (such as a warm pink or red), or
- For a schoolroom s/he would probably select a color suggesting intellectual activity but physical docility, such as a pale yellow.

Once the selection of the dominant color were completed, she or he could get to the fun part: selecting other colors to go with the base. That's where the rest of this chapter leads you.

COMPLEMENTARIES AND INSULTS

There are essentially six *intrinsically harmonious* color relationships, and one *intrinsically discordant* one, that can be used in various ways to achieve a desired interior or exterior effect. Each of them works by balancing two conflicting design elements: visual *tension* and visual *relaxation.* Notice that neither tension nor relaxation is necessarily positive or negative; each mood has its place, and each is used in good design.

(Please notice also that the word "complementary"—meaning "working together" is not the same as the word "complimentary," meaning "saying nice things about"; the use of the word "insults" above is a feeble effort at a defining joke.)

For this discussion, remember the pigment color wheel—its three primary colors (red, yellow and blue); its three secondary colors (green, orange, and purple), its six tertiary colors (yellow orange, yellow green, blue green, blue violet, red violet, and red orange), and the three "other colors": brown (and its extensions, such as tan and ebony); black (the perceived absence of all colors caused by their physical presence), white (the opposite of black) and the infinite range of greys. The twelve colors around the wheel, plus the browns (which can integrate with any of the other colors, since it includes them all) and greys (likewise) constitute the palette of the designer.

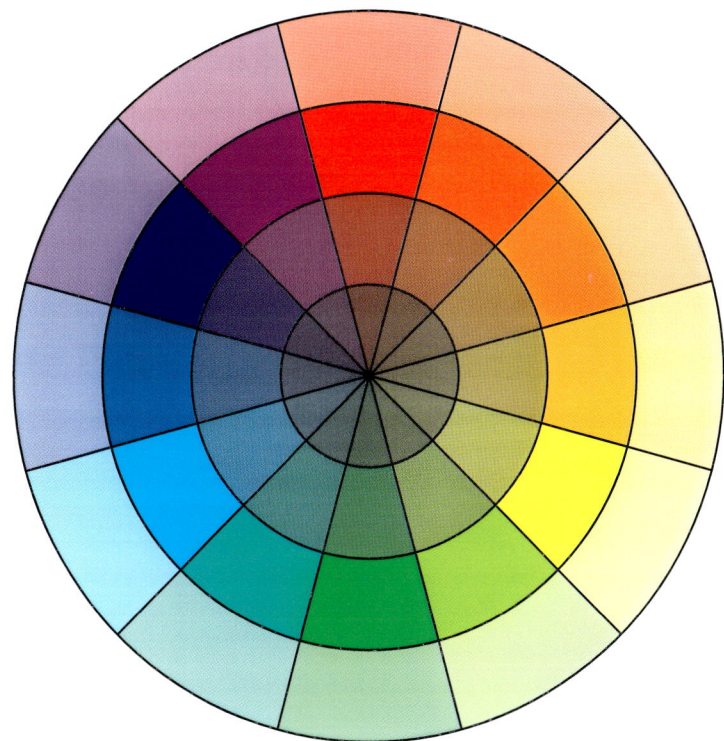

As a *footnote* (heh heh), the previous paragraph explains why beige remains the most popular color for carpet and other *flooring*. Since it *contains* all colors in a whitened and neutered form, it *harmonizes* with all colors equally well. The inexperienced would-be designer, such as the homemaker, intuitively selects beige because he or she knows it will be safe. And he or she is right, but the result will be less than interesting—which is why there are real designers, after all.

The seven color schemes possible with the fifteen hues are as follows:
- **Monochromatic,** in which only one hue is employed in various values of light and dark; this produces the greatest sense of restfulness and relaxation possible with a given hue.

- **Analogous,** in which two or more hues that reside side-by-side on the color wheel are employed together; this produces effects much the same as the monochromatic scheme.

- **Complementary,** in which two colors opposite each other on the color wheel are used together; this produces a greater feeling of tension than the monochromatic or analogous methods. Notice that if the selected colors are "pure" or "simple" (such as a saturated primary) the effect will be cartoonish; if the colors are more subtle—tertiaries, for example—the effect can be quite sophisticated.

- **Split complementary,** in which a color is used along with the *two* colors that reside *next* to the original color's complement on the wheel; this is both interesting and potentially stressful.

- **Triadic,** in which three hues evenly spaced on the color wheel are used together; again, please compare the difference between triadic primaries and triadic tertiaries.

- **Tetradic (double complementary),** in which two *pairs* of complementary hues, usually with one dominant and the other three subdued or used as accents.

- **Discordant,** in which widely separated non-complementary colors are used together to generate a feeling of great tension.

Let us go then, you and I, when the evening is spread out against the sky, like a patient etherized upon a table, and go make our visit to various sorts of rooms. Here we can see what is possible with these various color schemes, considering how they work and make some oversimplified generalizations about their use in Interior Design and Architecture. But remember—this is offered as an introduction, not pretended to be an education.

A *monochromatic* color scheme is used in places where the primary design concern is maintaining a specific mood. The values can range from saturated to tints or shades; whatever the psychological effects of the hue chosen, this scheme will exacerbate the effect. Thus, a room in tones of sand and beige will be calming to the point of soporificity; a room in tones of blue will feel like an aquarium; a room in tones of orange will resemble an amusement hall or the gates of Hades.

Here's an example of such a *monochromatic* color scheme.

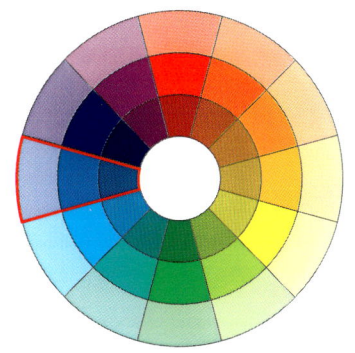

A *monochromatic* color scheme
using only tones of blue

An *analogous* scheme varies both the value and the hue of the colors used. Thus, they might be yellow, yellow-green, green, blue-green, and so on. The goal is to increase *and expand* the effects of the colors, and the direction taken by the diversion from the primary is itself important. For example, if you start with yellow and move in the direction of blue (as suggested above) you get one effect; if you start with yellow and move instead in the opposite direction—toward red—you get a very different effect. In a restaurant once adjacent to Chicago's Merchandise Mart, of the Present Author's experience, the walls were decorated with plywood cutouts in the shape of long tongues of flame painted in shades of orange and red; the room had an exciting, satanic name. A few years later, visiting the same space, the plywood shapes had been painted in tones of green, and the decorative theme of the restaurant restyled as a peaceful jungle. The *shapes* had remained the same, but because the direction of the changes-from-yellow directions of the analogous on the color wheel had changed, the whole room had a totally different feeling.

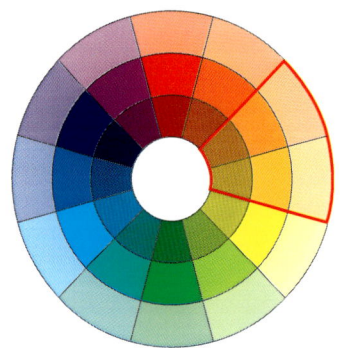

An *analogous* color scheme
using beiges, reds and oranges

A *complementary* scheme employs two colors opposite each other on the color wheel, which could be a primary and a secondary or two tertiaries. Almost certainly, they would not be used at the same *value,* unless a specific dynamic purpose (such as advertising) were intended; in the coloration of the interior or exterior of a structure one of the colors would be more *saturated,* and the other either darker or lighter in *value.* Theoretically, this pairing could also be done with a true hue and one or more brown shades, but that's stretching the term somewhat.

In real-world Interior Design complementary *tertiary* pair schemes are the most common; for example, yellow-orange and blue-purple are less discordant than red and green (unless tension is desired—think the traditional decorations for the winter holiday season). Complementary pairs are considered the least sophisticated of the color scheming methods.

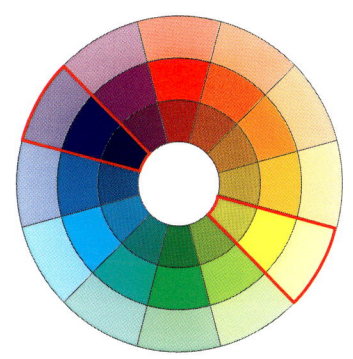

A *complementary* color scheme using blues and yellows

A *split complementary* scheme is much more interesting. To most architects and designers, green is the complement of red, and the resulting complementary relationship is (as noted above) inextricably tied to a specific event in the year. But green paired with red-orange and purple-red has no such connotations, and offers much more artistic tension. Yellow plus purple (a complementary scheme) is far less interesting than yellow plus purple-red and blue-purple. And notice again that things can be altered further by changing the *values* of one or more of the colors: a pale yellow-orange as the base color in a space, coupled with accents in saturated blue and purple, would be dynamic and exciting.

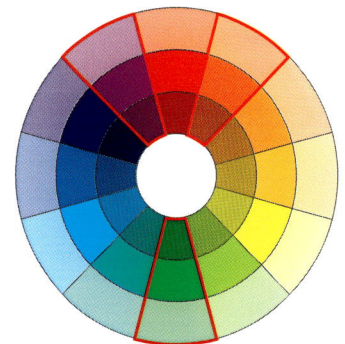

A *split complementary* color scheme using purples, green and oranges

A *triadic* scheme uses three hues evenly spaced around the 12 positions of the color wheel, such as purple-red, blue-green, and yellow-orange. Again, the designer almost certainly would vary the intensities of the hues, so that one (presumably the one occupying the largest area) would be the faintest in values, and the others used as accents.

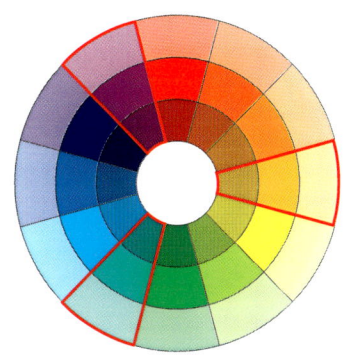

A *triadic* color scheme using blue-green, red-purple and yellow-orange

A *tetradic* of double complementary color scheme is difficult to pull off, because the presence of four colors can appear chaotic unless a firm hand establishes one as dominant. The complementary pairs of colors should not appear as an equilateral "X" across the color wheel, either, for the same reason; rather there should be one intervening hue between each of the two pairs, as a yellowish orange and a reddish orange along with a cool blue and a warmer one. There should be only one or, at most, two saturated colors; two or three should be tints, shades, or pastels.

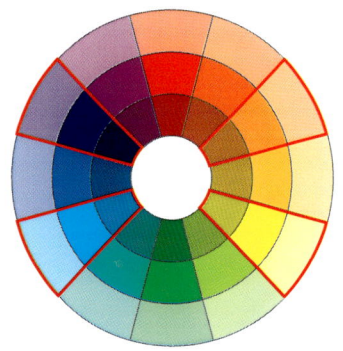

A *tetradic* color scheme using purple and yellow, with cyan and orange

A *discordant* color scheme is most likely to be encountered in a Postmodern interior, or another place where tension rather than harmony is the design goal. In this system, two or more colors that are widely separated on the color wheel are forced together, such as yellow and blue-green, or purple and red-orange. Since the effect is intended to be jarring, it is not uncommon for both hues to have the same value, further increasing the shock effect, although this is far from essential; with one or more hues muted, the effect changes but the tension does not. In this case, again, it takes skill to keep the outcome from looking like mere incompetence.

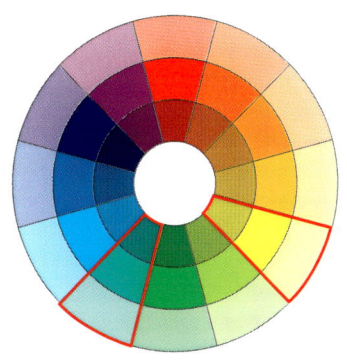

A *discordant* color scheme using yellow and blue-green

APPLICATION OF PRINCIPLES

The best part of all this is, of course, the fact that the Interior Designer or Architect can use the tools of hue, value, and relationship to produce a virtually endless stream of responses on the part of the viewer. Many of these responses—especially the ones dealing with psychotropic (acting on the mind) effects of color—are dealt with in the last Chapter of this book. But a few others—equally psychological, although less intimately affective—need discussion here. They relate to how the Architect or Interior Designer can use color to manipulate perceptions of space and the objects within that space. There are three principal ways color can help: by helping achieve balance or imbalance, by changing perceived size, and by altering the way people move within the space.

These effects are achieved because hue and value have another perceived character not yet described in this book: their energy and value can make objects appear to advance (by having energy) or recede (by seeming to be enervated or effete, or even by appearing to drain energy from other sources). Not surprisingly, these are directly related to the actual energy level of the individual color: the more active wavelength colors (reds and yellows) appear to advance or be larger, and the longer wavelength colors (blue and purple) appear to recede.

[Parenthetically, you may notice that when we discuss the combinations of colors we observe that brown—the sum of all colors—works with all other colors because it shares in their chromatic natures. You will also notice that we are now observing that green—the color in the *center of the spectrum*—neither advances nor recedes. A moment's reflection reveals that brown and green are the dominant colors of nature—trees and grass and plants in the forest. This can't be an acquired response, since the causes are mechanical and the consequences psychological. What is this instead—an interesting coincidence? A sign of Design? Something to ponder, Gentle Reader.]

Balance and imbalance

Since some colors advance and others recede, a designer can achieve visual balance by combining a larger object in a receding color (a pale blue, for example) and another object in a more intense, advancing color (a dynamic orange, for example). In the resulting complementary scheme, the eye would be pleased with the apparent balance while intrigued by the dissimilarities, and beauty could be the result.

In the same way, the designer could take three objects of identical size and color them in subtle complementary or triadic tones and achieve imbalance. Again, this would produce a pleasing disharmony within harmony that would captivate and enlighten.

If these principles are applied to a series of spaces within a total environment, the mood and character of each area can be established or modified while maintaining the design integrity of the whole project. This is a high goal of much Interior and Architectural design.

Perceived sizes

If a color or hue can make something appear to advance or retreat (and it can), then it follows that the apparent size of an object or a space can be modified by the application of color. And so it can: Just as the ranges of ever-more-distant mountains turn lighter and bluer on the horizon, so do lighter and bluer colors recede from the viewer, and more intense (more saturated) and warmer colors advance. Therefore, a large room could be made to seem less cavernous if painted in a deep red, or a small room less cramped if painted in a pale blue or green. (Of course, these *effect* goals can be overcome by the *fashion* goals of any particular moment, but that's another story.)

Contrast between colors or hues also introduce tension here. If the lower part of a room were given a dark, saturated warm hue, while the upper portion a cool, pale, recessive hue, the resulting discordance would be either nerve-wracking or invigorating, depending upon the skills of the designer.

Directing or controlling motion

Color can be used as a directional aid (as in using stripes on the floors or walls to lead people from one point to another), of course; that is discussed elsewhere in this book. But color selection can do more. Most people, presented with a choice of three differently colored open doors or archways, choose the one with the most open, receptive colors. But that does not mean the same thing all the time. there is a difference between involvement and commitment (as in the old joke that if you had bacon and eggs for breakfast a hen was involved but a pig was committed). Let's see how this applies to colors in the environment.

When it comes to making a commitment—for example, having to choose between a door opening into a red room, a bright yellow room, or a pale green room, most people will examine the brightly colored rooms but enter the pale green room first. The threat represented by the more "advancing" rooms seems to be off-putting.

But this does not apply to all forms of decoration. When presented with smaller objects—things that can be picked up, for example—or attractive objects (such as carpet samples in a retail store), people tend to go to the brighter colors before the duller, more recessive ones. Psychologically, it is as if brighter smaller objects "jump into the hand," while quieter larger spaces "invite the observer in." So, the designer—whether architect or Interior Designer—will use a combination of things that advance and withdraw as a way of guiding or forcing people through an area.

POSITIVE AND NEGATIVE SPACE

The work of Designers and Architects focuses both on the things they design and color (things that *are,* called "positive space") and the areas between the things that are (the places where things *aren't),* called "negative space." This concept is harder to articulate than understand. Please consider the following graphic:

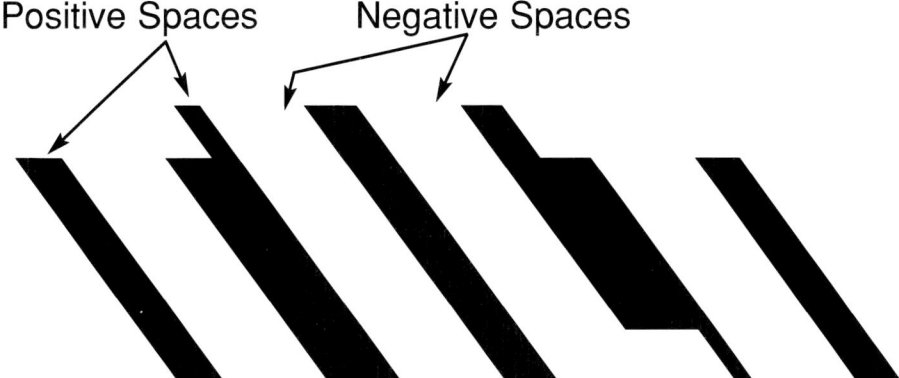

***POSITIVE AND NEGATIVE SPACES**—Look closely until you see the "hidden" word—the message is in the space between the objects—the "negative" space.*

CONCLUSION

This chapter does not pretend to have given you all you need to know to understand the complicated and interrelated worlds of the Interior Designer and architect. Its only purpose, as stated up front, is to give you a better sense of what these professionals do when they specific colors for a space, and a sense of the principles they employ in doing their work. And a quick visit to the studio or office of any of thee professionals will show you that they violate these "rules" as often as they follow them. But now you at least know what the rules *are,* and will be able to appreciate the skill of people who can employ them effectively.

Enjoy!

"Beauty isn't worth thinking about; what's important is your mind. You don't want a fifty-dollar haircut on a fifty-cent head."
—Garrison Keillor

CHAPTER 4
COLOR TRENDS AND TRENDING

"The same costume will be

Indecent	10 years	before its time
Shameless	5 years	" " "
Outré (daring)	1 year	" " "
Smart		
Dowdy	5 years	after its time
Hideous	10 years	" " "
Ridiculous	20 years	" " "
Amusing	30 years	" " "
Quaint	50 years	" " "
Charming	70 years	" " "
Romantic	100 years	" " "
Beautiful	150 years	" " " "

—James Laver

COLOR TRENDS AND TRENDING
▲ THE WHEEL IN THE SKY KEEPS ON TURNING ▲

Anyone worth his or her salt in a design-based business or industry wants to know what trends (including all aspects of fashion, such as color) are likely to be coming down the pike. This knowledge is essential to success, because in life change is inevitable, and there are only two ways of relating to it: either you control it, or it controls you. *Controlling change* is what *predicting trends* is all about.

And, as we have seen throughout this book, color is one of the most important aspects of any tangible object, such as a room, piece of furniture, or item of decor. It is the first thing people see when they look at the object or space, and (as you will learn in Chapter 6) the color(s) they see profoundly affect the way they feel about it. The reaction is so strong that it can become associated with specific memories of time and space. This means that a color that today seems new and trendy at some future date will be a weight pulling the mind back to the present, and that designing a space for tomorrow will require very different colors than those used in designing one for today. Therefore, predicting color trends in interior design (and, increasingly, architecture) is all the more vital.

With that having been said, there also must be a *caveat:* understanding and controlling trends of any kind, and color trends in particular, for almost any aspect of business is very difficult. In fact, for reasons we shall soon discuss, it is almost beyond the grasp of most organizations. But, as we shall also see, that is not as bad as it seems. In fact, in a paradoxical way, it is almost liberating. Let's see why.

THE "WHY" OF TRENDS

Trends of change in fashion, style, and design are not inevitable. In fact, they are almost contrary to normal human intuition, which tends to be more *conservative* (that is, adhering to the trends and patterns of the past) than *progressive* (desiring and instituting change). Examples demonstrating this observation are too obvious to need much enumeration, but here are a few:

- Patterns of tribal rugs ("Oriental" rugs) in Arabia and Persia have persisted virtually unchanged for centuries (as have the other habits and beliefs of the tribe members);

- Homes in once-isolated villages in The Netherlands such as Volendam or Urk had such distinct architecture and interior design (right down to the patterns used for the lace curtains) that a visitor could tell instantly from which town a photo was taken.

(In the last century progressivism due to globalization eroded this homogeneity, of course). Similarly, towns in the United States had similarly idiosyncratic architectures and colorings until recently. Consider the facing photograph: any reasonable person would recognize these as typical houses from the United States' New England.

- Even languages themselves persist in pronunciation and grammar when removed from outside influences—people in isolated regions of Appalachian North America persisted in speaking 18th Century English well into the late 20th Century, and their music was essentially unchanged from that of their Celtic forebears—compare the bluegrass music of the United States to the tunes and texts of songs by contemporary bands like The Chieftans (Irish) or the Battlefield Band (Scots).

In short, if people are allowed to remain undisturbed long enough to stew in their own juices, they tend to establish certain tastes and designs; these become "codes" or styles marking the members of a group or tribe. Once they have established these patterns they tend to preserve them. (See *Shibboleths and Shorthand, Natural Feelings, Unnatural Acts* and *Intelligent Lemonade* for other considerations of this phenomenon, including its implications and applications to communications).

What is the source of this desire to establish patterns and the resistance to changing them? Probably, two distinct factors drive it:

- The first is Newton's First Law of Motion: an object at rest tends to remain at rest, or an object in motion tends to remain in that motion, unless it is disturbed by an outside force. For social trends, this may mean that the simple prejudice of all organisms is to persist in whatever condition, maintaining whatever styles, fashions or colors they have (once such patterns have been developed) in order to avoid entropy (the loss of energy in any change of state).

- And the second factor driving the tendency toward stability in taste and fashion is more pedestrian but no less powerful: change costs money. Selling the perfectly good curtains you have and replacing them with new ones is expensive. This, of course, is merely another expression of Newton's law: spending money is another way of wasting energy.

Please consider this photograph as an example of the essentially conservative nature of human psychology. The architecture of these houses clearly shows they are characteristic of New England, where steep roof pitches are required to handle heavy snow and narrow overhangs allow sunlight into gloomy rooms. This is a fine example of the persistence and continuity of design, and the economies they afford: are we in a mill town in Lowell, Massachusetts? Fall River, Rhode Island?

In reality, these houses were built in Newry, South Carolina, where there is no snow and the sun needs to be kept away by extended shading overhangs, by textile mill owners who simply carried the blueprints in their carpet bags when they moved their plants away from unionized labor; the styles are consistent, regardless of where they were (however stupidly) executed, and the persistence of memory (without melted watches) affirmed. By the way—did you know that the "New England" village in the Harrison Ford movie Mosquito Coast *actually is Rome, Georgia?*

Counter to the natural tendency to stability and perpetuation of design patterns run four forces, which can be grouped into two categories. The first category is *internally driven* change—change that is desired by the individual who initiates it—and the second is *externally driven* change—change that is imposed on a group or society, often by another individual, but also possibly the result of nature, accident, or large social movements. The difference between these forces is universally recognized—in Arabic, for example, they are referred to as *"taghier,"* which means, "change from within," and *"taghir,"* which means "change by force." Notice how close these words are in sound—and how cosmically apart they are in meaning. (There is no comparable useful pair in English.)

Internally *driven change* can occur for any of three reasons:

- To correct an undesirable state of affairs (there is no English word for this condition, either; the Hopi word *koyaanisqatsi,* which means "A state of life so out of balance as to call for another way of living," popularized in the eponymous Godfrey Reggio/Philip Glass movie, is used as a shibboleth to express this concept);

- To express individuality or rebellion, as in scratching your name on the wall of a cave or the surface of a school desk, or

- Out of curiosity, restlessness, or mere boredom—a desire to discover what's on the other side of the mountain or what happens when you mix two chemicals. This is the source of both Galileo and *Jackass, the Movie.*

Externally *driven change* can occur for either of two reasons:

- The will to power (which Nietszche proposed also was the root of all architecture); the desire of an individual to impose his or her desires *on other people* and/or shout out the fact of his/her existence to a populated cosmos (which includes the fact that other people must react to the despoilment of graffiti or the name scratched on a wall or desk, or

- Someone's desire to make money, which usually means taking it from other people in some way, either socially useful or otherwise.

Let's consider these five possibilities in the context of their two broad categories. And let's remember that not even the chameleon changes colors because it's been placed on a new surface—everyone does it for one of these reasons.

First, there is the need to change because one finds oneself in an undesirable state of affairs. Granted, this can be considered externally-driven rather than internally-driven. Here, however, we are focusing on the response more than the stimulus, and different people can tolerate different amounts of unpleasantness. More important, this really isn't important to a discussion of trends, since once the situation is corrected the desire to change is removed. In short, individual responses to unpleasant circumstances don't lead to trends.

Next, there are the two non-essential reasons for internally-driven color change: boredom and the desire to make a personal statement. Boredom occurs primarily in weak, inner-directed societies, where people don't have the opportunity to do important new things. Since the motivation is inner-directed, so is the response; most people simply recolor themselves, their clothes, or their hair, and have no effect on others. (If they *do* affect others—if their ideas become a model or pattern—they no longer are inner-directed, obviously; for more about that, see below).

The same is true of the desire to make a personal statement that affects only the individual. As long as it is a personal statement, it is not an agent of change to the society and therefore is not a trend; it is an accident or a freak of nature (*lusus naturæ*).

Far more interesting are the desires to rebel or to make an individual statement for its own sake (which really are two sides of the same coin) that affect other people, especially if they attract a following. This desire is very important, because it calls out the natural Newtonian antipathy to itself. This is the desire of a group of people (almost always the young, whether merely chronologically young or truly young in spirit) to find ways to distinguish themselves from their parents and, by extension, their parents' tribal customs. Thus, many rebellious teenagers wear their hair, clothes or jewelry in ways designed to offend their parents' sensibilities: the success of a new purchase is the anguish of the parent's cries when beholding it. This tendency introduces new elements into the culture, and some of them become incorporated into the establishment.

Alternatively, young people can rebel so much that they leave their home turf and establish new tribes of their own, where their tastes can become the traditional cultures of those who remain within their purview. This influence can affect color, too: if enough young people decide they like a particular shade of green, and that can be sufficiently offensive to their parents, it may become part of their world.

While the rebuttal or individualistic force has potential to change tastes, it still must overcome the competing tendency for stability—again, Newton's First Law of Motion that things at rest tend to remain at rest unless acted upon by an outside force. The reasons for this in social terms are complex (mostly having to do with values acquisition, self actualization, and maintenance of the family structure in times of developing sexuality) but the evidence of the statement is all around—again, consider the fact that continuity, rather than diversity, is the hallmark of most societies, from the colors of Scots tartans to the ritual skin paintings of Native American Indians. In short, even though there are cultural tendencies leading to change in color, there are greater influences keeping those tendencies in check.

But a quick survey of any advanced (read: "like ours") society shows that instead of being stable, colors change at an amazing and almost alarming rate. A quick look at the racks of any consignment shop or Goodwill store shows hundreds of articles of clothing in excellent shape, yet being sold at a fraction of their new cost. The reason is that they "look outdated"—and the look often has less to do with style or cut than color.

This is the *mercantile* element driving trends and changes in color. If the desires to appear different, to do something new, to distinguish one's self from one's parents can be made to seem *important* in some way, people can be convinced to relinquish something perfectly usable because it no longer serves the purpose of appearing *current.* This is a "need" as valid and powerful as any other, more "practical" need driving a decision-making process.

And the manufacturers of stylish products are more than willing to indulge it, because changes in color cost virtually nothing, and yet they can move an object from desirable to undesirable in a matter of moments, and advance the "planned obsolescence" upon which a consumption-based society depends. The alternatives—imposing incompatible technological improvements (Pentium chips trumping 486 processors, or CDs supplanting LPs, for example), or making products that break rapidly and need replacement simply because of their shoddy construction—is far less honorable than the system of making things that merely turn ugly.

And that is why the colors of consumables change. Driven partly by the young's desire to appear new and distinctive, and encouraged by manufacturer's desires to sell new stuff, the natural desire to continue wearing that jacket, keep the perfectly-sound carpet, or avoid the hassle of reupholstering a chair can be overcome, and is overcome every day. And it is important to remember one last time that this is not an *organic* tendency; it is one that is *driven by intellectual forces.* From these understandings it's easier to build an appreciation of trends, trending, and the patterns in color preference over time.

OF THE NATURE OF COLOR TRENDS

Now that we realize that color trends are intellectually (rather than organically or naturally) driven, we can begin to consider the logic by which the process proceeds—since we know there eminently *is* a logic at work.

Manufacturers of products operate under certain constraints imposed by the psychological impact of colors when they design things (see the "Psychology of Color" chapter for more information). Some products need to make a "statement" which is better supported by some colors than others.

Manufacturers of electronics, such as stereo components, for example, tend to think of them as complex machines and therefore want a modern high-tech look, which leads them to select blacks, silvers, and other "non colors" for their products. This is an *external constraint* that directs their selection. But this constraint is far from fixed or universal: for years, stereo (or "high-fi") equipment was thought of as a *sort of musical instrument,* rather than a type of machine; in those days, amplifiers and speakers were wood-toned, with gold and brown colors on the face plates and façades. In other words, the color chosen was limited by the image the manufacturers desired to project, which itself was (and is) limited by the ideals and self-images of the age.

And these tend to be cyclic, too, in part because eventually the repetition of the same base colors leads to precisely the same sort of continuity that the whole idea of color change is designed to avoid. Thus, cameras were black and silver when first introduced to the masses at the beginning of the last century; over time, the proportion of black to silver increased, until by the end of the century many cameras were all black. At the turn of the 21st Century, the desire for change seems to be leading in three directions: a warm, honey-tone metal is starting to replace the silver on many cameras, others are starting to use sharp, harder metallic colors to accent the steel and aluminum colors of the bodies—and black and silver is back, too.

In the preceding paragraph we also met one of the truly essential words in any study of color: *cycles.* The range of practical raw materials available limits colors, like everything else; the spectrum includes only a limited number of distinct hues, so the same colors will come and go. The less constrained an industry is by external limitations (such as the electronics industry's current need to appear high-tech), the more rapid the change can be. And since rapid change is tied to increased profits, the more rapid color changes *will* be in those industries, and the more rapidly the cycle from color to color will pass.

In fashion and home furnishings (the intended audience of this little article, of course), change occurs fairly rapidly. Combining the *generational* factor (children looking for something new), *mercantile* factor (the manufacturer's desire to make perfectly usable current things appear out-of-date), the *resistance* factor (most people's natural conservatism) and the *practicality* factor (the limitations placed by budgets on most people's discretionary purchases), the end result is a cycle time of roughly one generation—about 25 to 30 years, in the United States at this time. In other words, the colors that your parents grew up with, which were radical and outlandish to their parents, will become the colors you like as you enter the same stage in your life. And since different people are being born and dying at different times, the flow from color to color will appear to be a steady, 25-year cycle, constantly repeating itself. Avocado was hot in 1975, and (heaven help us all) it's coming back again.

But not quite the same. The avocado of 25 years ago is not quite the same as the funky greens of 2005. That's because the people *designing* the green are responding to a slightly different ethos or *Weltanschauung*. More about that below.

What we have, therefore, is a sort of Yeatsian *gyre*. William Butler Yeats (the Irish poet) described a view of history in which events occurred, not in a circle, but on a spiral that he called a "gyre," so that every time a full 360º of change had been achieved the whole plane of the circle had advanced (and diminished or increased in diameter, but that's another story). In the same way, the colors used in a fashion industry revolve and evolve, so that a particular color is hot, then cold, then hot again—but the *new* "hot" version of the color is different in subtle ways from the version that was hot the *last* time.

The student of trends therefore needs to be sensitive to two different sets of issues—what colors are coming back, and what form (bright, dull; simple, complex; clear, muddy) are they taking. This kind of understanding—only slightly more complex than merely looking at the trends themselves—will equip the Gentle Reader to predict the future. However, before getting too carried away with this, the Gentle Reader must also learn one more fact: this knowledge is useful only to a certain degree, and helpful only as long as it is used appropriately.

THE DARK TRUTH: THE ANGST OF TREND SPOTTING

This chapter has tried to give you some insights into the way trends develop and what forces drive them. But it also reveals three reasons why this very kind of study should not consume too much of the Gentle Reader's or Present Author's time.

This is a look backward—but is it also a glimpse of the future? Hem lines, hair styles, and head gear come and go, up and down; perhaps the most important truth to remember is, "Never say 'never again'!"

The first reason is our old friend the mercantile impulse, mentioned above. The second reason is the dynamic, almost organic nature of the change cycle. And the third is the actual job requirements of the Gentle Reader and Present Author: while we should understand the trends, and know the reasons and principles underlying them, we should not forget that we are not responsible for their design—only supporting their implementation. That is not intended to sound pessimistic, and is not; it is, however, a chance to get something more out of the work that each of us does. Let's consider these three factors individually.

Reason One: people far away make the marketing decisions

The people who make the things that are used to make the things that have colors largely direct the process of making the colors that the things have. And these people have a very important extra function in the scheme of things: making certain that the things that people make with the stuff they make makes sense.

That intentionally clumsy paragraph is intended to point up that the companies who produce things for other manufacturers—just as DuPont produces fibers for carpet manufacturers—have great control over the colors that will be used by the manufacturers themselves. If all the dye producers in the world suddenly decided to stop making red dye, there would be no more red products. When DuPont decides to produce a line of solution-dyed fibers, those colors become the *de facto* standard for the industry. And colors produced by other means—such as beck or continuous dyed carpets—tie into the producer-supplied stuff, or wander off at their own peril.

And the peril is very real, because the chief suppliers to an industry tend to dominate more than one manufacturer. When Microsoft eats a hot dog, the computer world gets heartburn; when a major fashion designer decides to show three inches of bare midriff, women all over the Western world get goose bumps—and not just from excitement.

This is a powerful force for good, because the continuity implied—or even enforced—by these decisions means that various manufacturers will have products that coordinate with each other. If DuPont makes a color, Steelcase will work with that color, and so will Knoll; thus, if Milliken makes a carpet it will coordinate with the upholstery fabrics made by Waverly or Scalamandra. The world of the Architect and Interior Designer, as well as the world of the consumer, benefit from this harmony—in reduced costs of design and production of goods, greater ease of decoration, increased speed of producing in-stock materials, and so on.

Thus, when DuPont makes a "Color Forecast" it is in many ways truly a self-fulfilling prophecy, and that is not necessarily a Bad Thing.

Reason Two: The dynamics of change

That change is inevitable is as certain as that change is resisted. When this immovable force runs headlong into its matching immovable object, as observed in the old song, "something's got to give," and what gives—what is the result—is the cyclical pattern of color trends. The Present Author has discovered what he perceives to be the nature of the cycles—there are two, one of which is the change from one color to the next, and the other is the change from saturated colors to muted colors and back again, and the two trends, read together, produce an accurate prediction of what lies ahead. However, this research is not complete, and therefore not included here. But that's not important, for another reason, which—again—comes courtesy of a major supplier to major suppliers.

It would be unseemly to identify the source of this observation, so let's refer to it as a representative of a Very Major Company. This person was asked directly by the Present Author on what basis the company made its forecasts, and s/he replied that they had a complex formula based on interviews and studies and (here the message got lost in the language). The Present Author paused and then asked, "Yes, but what do you do really?" The other person stared directly in the Present Author's eyes, paused, and then said, "What they are wearing in Paris or Milan this year they will be wearing in New York and Los Angeles next year, and that will be on their furniture the year after, and on their floors the year after that."

The present author looked back and said "Wow!" The Other Person then paused again and continued, "Do you want the shorthand version? Open a fashionable woman's closet today. Look at the colors. That's what will be in the house in two year's time."

Take it for what you think it's worth, Gentle reader, and if you take it for little, please conclude with the next section.

Reason three: The Difference between Tactics and Strategy

There is a natural tendency in any conscientious member of an organization to want to aspire upward—to concern himself or herself with the issues driving the organization. That's a natural part of being a good Employee, Associate, Colleague or Team member (whatever jargon your particular employer is using at the moment). This is identification with the *strategic* or long-term issues of the organization. But it is important to remember that in most organizations the power to make those decisions is closely guarded by the people who have achieved the empyrean positions of power for which they have strived most of their lives, and it's about as unlikely that they will share those powers with a lowly serf as that Tutankhamen will be dancing at your holiday party.

In other, more direct and unkind words, the decision-making activity in a company like yours is done by the people who provide the products—the designers and colorists. Just as they are at the mercy of the fiber people, the street-level worker is at their mercy.

Does this mean that you have no role in long-term forecasting? Of course not. If that were the case this chapter would not have been written. Your role is to understand the trends in the industry, understand the color philosophies of your organization, understand how color can be used to achieve your clients' goals, and—armed with this information—represent the products that you have to use to the best of your abilities. Informed, informing, and informational, you will be the essential asset upon which your customers—both internal and external, both upward and downward in the chain—depend. And that *will* be a Good Thing.

SO, AFTER SUCH KNOWLEDGE, WHAT FORGIVENESS? IS THERE ANYTHING TO BE LEARNED ABOUT TRENDING?

Obviously, the answer is "yes." The smart communicator who works in the fields of style and color does six things:

- Learns what external Customers need in the way of product and color;

- Feeds this information back into the system by passing it up the chain;

- Understands how the internal and external Customers communicate (see *Shibboleths and Shorthand, Natural Feelings, Unnatural Acts, The Interior Design Reference Book,* and *Intelligent Lemonade* for more information about how to do this;

- Predicts what colors are likely to be forthcoming from your suppliers (internal and external);

- Knows how to read the signs of trend shifting so you can position what your suppliers need in terms of what your customers need in the way that they want, and

- Reaps the rewards of these successes.

And how do you do this?

- First, yes, study the color forecasts. DuPont makes them available. This will allow the person to speak with confidence and authority.

- Speak to the designers in the company. Listen to their vocabularies, memorize their words, and repeat them. This will give a sense of communion with customers, who are hearing the same words from other vendors.

- Learn how to forecast. Remember, what's on the street in Madrid or Amsterdam will be in the closet in the US in two years and in carpet two years later. The Cliff's Notes version of the shorthand sentence is "In no more than four it's on the floor."

And, at the same time, remember that home furnishings are more traditional, more greyed and subtle than clothes—a $300 dress can be replaced with less concern than a $5000 carpet. Therefore, the chartreuse jacket you bought will be more like the avocado we mentioned by the time it gets to home furnishings—or the home furnishings may merely be colored to work well with it as part of a design scheme (see Chapter 3). Finally, remember that the cycle will be a spiral, not a wheel. But that will prepare you for the future. Enjoy getting to know it—it's where you're going to have to live.

"Where are we going? and why am I in this hand-basket!"

—Anonymous

CHAPTER 5
A Color Glossary

"Writing about music is like dancing about architecture."

—Frank Zappa

A Color Glossary
▲ 7,689 Words and No Pictures ▲

One of the hardest parts of talking about color is getting a shared understanding of exactly what the terms—and, especially, the names of various colors—actually mean. The following glossary addresses part of this problem by providing definitions of key terms used in the discussion of color, color production, and color measurement. For efficiency, terms used in the list that are defined elsewhere are printed in CAPITAL LETTERS. However, the issue of discussing the *names* of the colors *themselves* remains.

There are three ways of approaching this problem:
- The first is printing swatches of various colors and labeling them. This approach has the advantage of providing clear descriptions, but the huge disadvantage of tying the descriptions to the specific perceptions of an author, or (only slightly better) a group of reviewers. The present book does not use this method because the Present Author lacks sufficient confidence in his own omniscience to feel comfortable matching hues and names in this way.
- The second is referencing competent authorities, such as various dictionaries and color encyclopedias, and using their terminologies to describe colors and allowing the Gentle Reader to translate the word pictures into personal apprehensions.
- The third, which (as far as the Present Author knows) has not been tried so far, is to arrange the names of various colors on a sort of "color spectrum," so that the Gentle Reader has a comparative sense of how colors may relate to each other. In other words, even though the writer and reader may have different ocular apparati, their idiosyncratic perceptions could be individually consistent enough to allow useful relative understandings.

The Present Author has opted for the latter choices, with the following consequences. You will please find here two indices. The first, which is alphabetical, gives definitions for many terms important in the discussion of color, as well as descriptions of various color names, as drawn from a chaotic mass of reference books to which the Present Author has gone for direction.

The second index is a little more unusual. It takes the words used to describe color and, in accordance with the principles mentioned above, arranges them in a Verbal Color Spectrum™, of which the Present Author is so foolishly proud that he has taken the liberty of protecting the name and concept. The Gentle Reader is invited to use this as much as possible to develop a sense of what these various words may mean.

Enjoy!

ADDITIVE (COLOR SYSTEM)—A light-based color system in which the primary hues of green, blue and red are added together.

ADOBE—As a building material, a sun-dried mud brick used primarily in the American Southwest; as a color, a pinkish brick red.

AFU—See AMERICAN FADE UNITS.

AFTERIMAGE—A visual phenomenon in which an image persists—in reversed tones—after the source has been removed, as when someone gazes intently at a drawing for some time, shifts her or his eyes to a white surface, and sees the original picture in reversed (COMPLEMENTARY) colors on the new plane. The afterimage is due to overstimulation of the visual apparati during the period of intense study. This is important in critical work areas: for example, surgeons in an operating room see afterimages of blood and gore when they shift their eyes, unless the room's decor anticipates and accommodates the problem.

ALUMINUM—A dull white METALLIC color.

AMERICAN FADE UNITS—The standard used for measuring a product's resistance to losing color *(fading)* due to ozone, swamp gas, or other problems. *Free* ozone in the lower atmosphere is *increasing* at the same time as the ozone *layer* in the upper atmosphere (which protects the earth from ultraviolet radiation is *deteriorating,* making attention to fade resistance ever more important. Typically, skein dyed yarns will hold color for 40 AFU hours, while solution dyed yarns have a minimal FASTNESS of 80 AFU, and 500 AFU is not uncommon.

ANALOGOUS (COLOR SCHEME)—A color palette based on two colors found side-by-side on the COLOR WHEEL, as blue or green and blue-green.

AQUA—A light greenish-blue color.

AURA—A pervasive presence in the air or atmosphere. It can be distinctive but intangible (as in an aura of dignity) or subtle but perceptible (as in an aura about her head); it is in this latter sense that it is important to the subject of color. See SPECTRUM and BIOPLASMIC ENERGY.

BIOPLASMIC ENERGY—The condition of living (*"bio"*) forms of a highly ionized gas (*"plasma"*) emanating from a (usually understood to be human) body. This is thought to be the source of *auras,* glowing "haloes" perceived by some people around the heads (and bodies) of other people; bioplasmic energy is claimed to be the source. For more information, please refer to *Design for Destiny* (Edward W. Russell), *Psychiatry and Mysticism* (edited by Stanley R. Dean), and the works of Faber Birren.

BLACK—The absence of color in the optical system, and the equal presence of all colors in the pigment system; lacking HUE and brightness and absorbing all light without reflecting any of the rays composing it.

BLACK BODY RADIATOR—See COLOR TEMPERATURE.

BLOOD RED—A deep, blackish CRIMSON color.

BLUE—The color of the sky; one of the three PRIMARY COLORS (falling between red and yellow on the COLOR WHEEL), the WAVELENGTH of which is between 450 and 500 nm (nanometers).

BRAINWASHING—The replacement of an individual's own personal value systems and beliefs with those of others. The process is associated with TOTALITARIAN regimes, and usually is accomplished by sensory deprivation, the application of drugs, psychological stress techniques, or torture. DESIGN, ARCHITECTURE, and CHROMOTHERAPY often are components of the mix; monotony is a powerful tool for erasing thought.

BRASS—A yellow METALLIC color, slightly redder than GOLD; also, a term for nerve or chuzpah.

BRONZE—A METALLIC brownish color.

BROWN—A color produced by mixing all three primary colors in various proportions. The specific hue is determined by which of the component(s) predominates. See the brown VERBAL SPECTRUM.

BURNT OCHRE—Brownish yellow-orange color; compare to OCHRE.

BURNT SIENNA—An intense dark reddish-brown color; compare to SIENNA.

BURNT UMBER—Deep, shadowy greyed yellow-reddish earth-brown color—both yellower and duller than burnt sienna. Compare to UMBER.

CALVIN—Not the same as KELVIN, which please see. John Calvin (1509-1564) was a French/Swiss Christian theologian who posited a theory of predestination based on his conclusion that God's will was perfectly worked out at the instant of creation, that what happened to every thing in creation must follow logically, and that therefore God must know everyone's ultimate end—including salvation or damnation. This view is positively optimistic when compared to that of the English philosopher Thomas Hobbes (1588-1679) who argued that all existence was a series of accidents, God was merely a First Cause, and "free will" and even "soul" were meaningless terms. These ideas were once articulated daily with brilliant whimsy in Bill Watterson's strip *Calvin and Hobbes,* and more darkly in Kurt Vonnegut's *Sirens of Titan.* See WAVE THEORY.

CELADON—An effete pale grey-green color.

CELERY—Pale yellowish green color; slightly less gloomy than CELADON.

CELSIUS—A temperature scale named for Swedish astronomer Anders Celsius, in which water freezes at 0° and boils at 100°, originally called "Centigrade" since it divides the interval between these two important and universal phenomena into 100 units; compare to KELVIN and see COLOR TEMPERATURE.

CERISE—Moderate to deep red—the colors of a cherry (French *cerise*).

CERUSE—A pigment composed of white lead; rather warmer than the whites of Zinc and Titanium. This is a very rare word, but serves to remind one that all whites are not the same—some are colder, some warmer, and so on. See COLOR TEMPERATURE.

CERULEAN BLUE—The color of the sky on a clear day, such as one of those upon which you can see forever—a brilliant, clear blue.

CHALK, CHALKY—When used to describe paint, it means weathered, dull, unSATURATED.

CHAMELEON—An animal—actually, to be more precise, either of two sorts of tree-dwelling lizards—with the remarkable ability to change color. The true chameleon (family *Chamæleontidæ,* suborder *Sauria,* genera *Brookesia* [16 species] and *Chamæleo* [68 species]) ranges from southern Spain, across Africa, into western Asia; the so-called "false chameleon" (a creature which suffers from terrible problems of self-esteem, no doubt) is the *Anolis Carolinensis,* of the family *Iguanidæ.* They grow from 7" to 10" long (except for a few that get up to 2'), have flat bodies, independently movable bulgy eyes, and specialized cells called *melanophores* containing granules of pigment (melanin, which also colors all forms of animal skin). Under the control of the autonomic nervous system, melanophores allow the animal to change color—depending upon the species, among green, yellow, cream, and dark brown—and pattern, such as stripes, spots, and blotches. Changes are determined not by background color (as is commonly assumed) but by the little critter's emotional state—anger, lust, fear, or simply asserting that it is MIBU™. See UNDERWEAR.

CHAMPAGNE—A very pale yellow with a hint of green.

CHARTREUSE—Clear light green with a yellowish cast, named for the liqueur of the same name. Look at it, but don't drink it.

CHOCOLATE—A very dark brown with a reddish, almost purplish cast.

CHROMA—The intensity or purity of a color; its freedom from TINTS or SHADES of grey or white.

CHROMODYNAMICS/CHROMOTHERAPY—The study of the powerful influence of color on individuals' mental state. In its simplest form, basic colors evoke basic emotions: red is exciting, green is restful, blue is cheerful (paradoxically), yellow stimulates action and thought, pink is pacifying and so on. Research shows certain larger recommendations: *workplaces* work best with a COMPLEMENTARY scheme of yellow, orange, or orange-yellow with pale blue or green; *concentrated mental activity* seems to work best in an environment of soft and moderately contrasted hues; *homes* should use various colors suitable for the rooms' activities; *stores* can stimulate sales with yellow tones and so on. Please see Chapter 6.

CINNAMON—Reddish brown color.

COBALT BLUE—Deep, strong greenish blue (see COBALT GREEN).

COBALT GREEN—Deep, strong bluish green (see COBALT BLUE).

COFFEE—Rich, reddish-brown color.

COLOR—See HUE.

COLOR BLINDNESS—The condition of having restricted, or no, ability to perceive color, to a degree greater than the normal variations between individuals.

Achromatopsia is the condition of being totally unable to distinguish colors, seeing things only in shades of grey; *commonly* known as "color blindness." The eye can see colors because of the presence in the eye of receptors called "cones" and "rods"; in the condition of achromatopsia, there are blocks or deficiencies in these receptors.

If the receptors are only partly deficient, the result is called *anomalous trichromatism,* a difficulty in distinguishing between colors that appear very different to most people. The most common "color blindness" is properly called *daltonism*. In the daltonic eye, cones that should be sensitive to a particular primary hue (a color which cannot be made by mixing two other colors) are, in fact sensitive to its *complementary* (that color which is "opposite" it on the color wheel, composed of the *mixture* of two adjacent primary colors). And, remember, there are two color systems: pigment, in which the primary colors are red, yellow, and blue, and the *optical* system, in which they are red, green, and blue-violet.

Thus, in the eye suffering from anomalous trichromatism, there will be various deficiencies. If the eye is insensitive to or lacks the red receptor, it is said to be *protanopic;* if the problem lies with the green receptor the eye is *deuteranopic,* and if the blue-violet receptor is deficient the eye is said to be *tritanopic*.

COLOR MATCHING—Coordinating HUES and tones in manufacturing or producing things. There are two critical elements in color matching: first, the *light under which the colors are compared* and, second, the *surface LUSTER* or TEXTURE of the objects being matched.

The Effect of Light on Color Matching. White light contains all of the colors in the rainbow, and an object placed under it absorbs all but its "own" color. Objects literally take their color from the light under which they are viewed. If a color is missing from the light, or present to a too high or low degree, the object can't reflect its "own" color correctly. For example, under the yellowish light of incandescent light bulbs, everything will look yellowish, because primarily yellow is available to be reflected. Under cool white fluorescent tubes, everything looks bluish. Under daylight, everything looks brighter. Therefore, it is imperative to state under which light source an object will be color **matched**. One common industry standard is the MACBETH LIGHT. See also OTT LIGHT.

The Effect of Texture on Color Matching. The surface texture of an object greatly affects its apparent color. A rough surface reflects light in more angles than a smooth one. In carpet this effect means that cut pile carpet, for example, will always appear darker than loop pile carpet made of the same yarn—again, because the light is absorbed and reflected differently. (See SHADING.)

In the same way, the LUSTER of the yarn will affect the apparent color; higher luster fibers will look lighter than other, lower luster fibers. But deepening the dye will still not produce an acceptable match, because is is not truly a *color* matching problem in such a case, but rather *luster* matching—which must be dealt with on its own terms.

COLOR TEMPERATURE—At first blush, this term must look like an oxymoron or simple error—how can an abstract entity have a physical existence, such as temperature? Why not weight, too? (For which, please see Chapter 6.) This term actually is a window into an important subject. The Gentle Reader must decide how far into this window she or he chooses to look; therefore, each of the following paragraphs is self-sufficient and subsequent paragraphs merely add more detail to what goes before. Stop whenever you've had enough.

As you know, color is both a mechanical and electrical phenomenon with ties to both worlds. The light under which color is viewed affects what the color looks like. Different light sources are described in terms of their *color temperature*—that is, "WARM" and "COOL" lights have certain "colors." If you know the color temperature of the light used when a particular comparison of hues was made, you can more accurately predict how accurately a similar comparison will work at another location.

Color temperature is measured in degrees Kelvin (°K). The range is from 8000°K (the harsh, bright white of a snowy day under a cloudless sky) to 2000°K (the deep orange of candle light). Here's a typical color scale:

	Outdoor Light Source	**Indoor Light Source**
8000°K	Snow, water under clear cloudless sky	
6500°K	A few clouds, large open sky	
5500°K	Average daylight in Morocco or Florida	A commercial photographer's XENON flash
	Average daylight in Maine or France	Standard strobe or blue flash
4500°K		Fluorescent tubes
	Early morning light Late afternoon	"Warm white" Fluorescent tubes
3500°K	Evening sunlight	
		Photofloods 150-Watt bulbs
	Dusk	100 Watt bulbs
2500°K	Sunset	60 Watt bulbs 40-Watt bulbs 25-Watt bulbs
2000°K		Candlelight

The first thing you will probably notice is, just as there are two sets of primary colors (one for optics and the other for pigments), there also are two opposite uses of the words "warm" and "cool," one for each system. A warm *light* is produced at a high-temperature color (such as blue) and a cold *light* is produced at a lower-temperature color (such as red). However, when referring to the *color of the light,* the terms are used as elsewhere in this book: a red light is "warm," and a blue light is "cool."

Next, you can see, most interior light bulbs (called *tungsten* bulbs because of the material of which the glowing filament is made) operate in the area of 3200°K, and therefore cast an orange (warm) glow on things. Most fluorescents operate around 4600°K and therefore cast a greenish-blue (cool) glow on things. These differences show up most clearly when photographing objects with film balanced for sunlight (around 5000°K). Correcting for these errors is easy by using an appropriate FILTER; an 80-A is used to correct daylight film for tungsten light, and an FL-D to correct it for fluorescent light.

The principle upon which this color temperature system is based is a theoretical model comparing the temperature of a hypothetical black object heated to various temperatures (imagine an iron bar) glowing brighter and brighter as the heat is increased, measured in degrees Kelvin (which is merely degrees Celsius [Centigrade] plus 273 degrees; thus, 1727°C equals 2000°K. At 900°K the iron glows a dull, cherry red; between 1500°K and 2000°K it turns orange; at 3000°K it is yellow-white, and at 5000°K it is bluish-white. This is called the **black body radiator** measurement.

To convert degrees Fahrenheit (°F) to Celsius (°C) subtract 32 and then multiply by 5/9 (or, in a pinch, halve it). Thus, 72°F equals 22°C (72-32=40; 40 x 5 = 200; 200/9 = 22.222), and also equals 295°K (by adding 273). To convert Celsius to Fahrenheit, multiply the temperature by 9/5 (or, in a pinch again, double it) and add 32. Thus. 3500°K—the color temperature of evening sunlight—equals 3227°C (3500 – 273) or 1812°F (3227/9 = 358.555; 356 x 5 = 1780; 1780 + 32 = 1812): a fairly warm iron bar, and coincidentally the date of Napoleon's disastrous attack on Moscow; see the Tchaikovsky overture of the same name (especially in the old Mercury "Living Presence" recording with Antal Dorati).

COLOR WHEEL—A circle showing the relationship between various colors or hues. It has three primary points, equidistant around the rim of the circle, for the three PRIMARY colors (red, yellow and blue, in the pigment system); between them are three points for the SECONDARY colors (orange, green and purple). The rest of the wheel consists of shades slipping from one hue to the next, making it possible to see the relationship between the colors. Brown sometimes is depicted at the center of the circle, with shades radiating outward to the rim; alternatively, the center can be black or white and the resulting "spokes" can show degrees of CHROMA and brown treated as a separate SPECTRUM. The whole is a visual representation of the spectrum in a useful learning method.

COMPLEMENTARY (COLOR SCHEME)—A palette-based on colors positioned exactly opposite each other on the COLOR WHEEL. Note the spelling.

COOLNESS—The degree to which a color tends toward the yellow/green side of the spectrum. Compare to WARMTH; also see HUE.

COPPER—A reddish metallic color; also a slang term for a penny (which is plated with the metal) and an old insulting name for a policeman. "What's an old penny made of?" "Dirty copper!"

CREAM—An off-white color, with a hint of yellow.

CRIMSON—Deep purplish red color.

CYAN—An important SHADE of blue; COOL, tending toward green, used as one of the three basic PRIMARY COLORS in printing operations.

DIFFUSE—To separate or split apart, as in light passing through a piece of FROSTED glass while the parallel rays that reveal the appearance of an object being scattered and the object rendered as a blurry shape rather than what it really appears to be.

DYE—As a noun, a substance containing PIGMENTS—coloring materials that can impart a HUE to another object or surface; as a verb, to employ such a noun. There are several sources for dyes:
- **Natural**—vegetable or mineral. These are the original dyes, used for centuries; they tend to fade and are inconsistent in color.
- **Aniline**—derived from coal tar or other sources of nitrobenzene; these dyes tend to be corrosive and unstable, and after their popularization around 1865 fell out of favor.
- **Acid**—derived from acidic groups, such as the sulfo group, used chiefly for silk and wool, tending to be cheap and liable to CROCK and BLEED.
- **Chrome**—derived from the dichromate of elements such as potassium or sodium, these relatively modern dyes are FAST and stable, and are widely used in ORIENTAL RUGS. Also please see HUE.

EBONY—A very deep brownish-black.

ECRU—A very light brown, like unbleached flour or linen.

EGGPLANT—Almost black purple color.

EUDEMONICS—The theory or art of happiness, from the Greek *eudaímōn* for "blessed with a good genius, fortunate, happy." The Present Author wishes eudemonia to the Gentle Reader.

FADING TEST—A test to predict the likelihood of carpet losing HUE under actual use conditions. Fading is usually caused either by ultraviolet light or exposure to ozone gas; the first is commonly found in any extremely sunny area, and the second in the presence of electrical storms or swamp gasses. Carpet can be tested in special chambers against either hazard. The specific HUE chosen for an application, the FIBER on which it is to be applied, and the CONSTRUCTION itself can all affect fadeability, so a specific carpet being considered for a critical installation should be tested prior to selection.

FILTER—Something through which another thing is passed for the purpose of altering it. Filters can screen out impurities (as in the air flow of a furnace), align or correct things (as in the filters in a phonograph amplification system), or change them from one form to another. It is this last sense that is important to optics; filters can change the characteristics of light and thereby the perceptions of the pigments under which it is viewed. Some filters are intentional (as in the filters used to balance the color TEMPERATURE of film) and some are inadvertent (as in the filtering of the color of light by incandescent or fluorescent light bulbs). This is an important subject of its own, but only peripherally important to the design professional—yet it needs to be understood in those rare occasions when it affects decision-making. See OTT and MACBETH lights.

FROSTED—When said of glass, the term means hazed or etched over with powders or acids so that the glass is TRANSLUCENT (permitting light to pass while DIFFUSING images) rather than TRANSPARENT.

FUCHSIA—A bright purplish red color; compare to MAGENTA. The word is pronounced "***fyoo***-sha."

GINGER—Yellowish or reddish brown color.

GOLD(EN)—A METALLIC color, rich yellow with a touch of brownish-green.

GOLDEN RECTANGLE, GOLDEN SECTION—A proportion used in all aspects of design. Discovered by the ancients, it can be computed by dividing a line so that the ratio of the whole to the larger part is the same as the ratio of the larger part to the smaller. An easier but much less scientific and less accurate way is to take a rectangle, draw a diagonal, and then take a perpendicular to the line to either of the other corners. Repeating the process will produce points which, if connected, will result in a smaller rectangle inside the larger one—in roughly the Golden Proportions.

GRAPE—Dull, dark purplish red color; obviously, this is both an approximation and a generalization, since real grapes shade from pale greens to almost black.

GREEN—The color of leaves, grasses and some ripening fruits; one of the three SECONDARY COLORS (a mixture of YELLOW and BLUE on the COLOR WHEEL), the WAVELENGTH of which is between 500 and 570 nm (nanometers).

GREY (GRAY)—The ultimate neutral—neither warm nor cold, dark nor light, intense nor subdued—made by mixing various amounts of black and white. Greys can be immensely complex and sophisticated, because neither black nor white is ever entirely pure, so various hints of tones can creep in to the grey. Grey is not on the *Verbal Spectrum,* therefore.

HENNA—Midway between red-brown and orange-brown.

HUE—What is commonly called "color," hue is a graduation or variety of a property by which the appearance of light or an object can be classified as red, green, yellow, or so on. An *object's* hue is determined by the light it *reflects*; it *absorbs* from the light all hues other than its "own." Hence, it is essential for *all* hues to be equally present in the light source if an accurate determination of the *object's* hue is to be made. (See COLOR MATCHING.)

    Hues are discussed in terms of their position in a light *spectrum* (plural "spectra"). Each hue has a *wavelength*—an electromagnetic vibration of a particular length measured in millionths of a millimeter (nm). The human eye can see only wavelengths between 380 nm (violet) and 780 nm (red). This defines the limits of the spectrum. In practice there are two types of spectra—one for light and the other for *objects.*

The **light spectrum** consists of three *primary hues.* (A primary hue is one that cannot be produced by combining other hues.) They are red, blue, and green. If you combine all three, you produce white light.

The **pigment spectrum** also consists of three primary hues: red, blue, and yellow. If you combine all three, you produce more or less black PIGMENT. Since pigment is the key element in carpet coloring, the rest of this article deals only with it.

There are three *secondary hues* in pigment, obtained by combining primary hues. Red and yellow produce orange, blue and yellow produce green, and blue and red produce purple. If the hues are "ideal" (magenta, cyan, and light cadmium yellow) and mixed evenly, they produce black. In reality, because of the WARMTH and COOLNESS of actual pigments, most yellows, reds and blues mixed together produce a muddy, greyish brown.

Each of the hues has a *complement*—a hue that goes well with it. The complementary colors are any primary color and the secondary color made up from the other two primaries. Thus, red and green, purple and yellow, and orange and blue are complementary.

Hues are derived from pigments that must bond to a fiber's DYE SITES. The pigments can be *natural* (organic or inorganic) or *synthetic.* Organic dyes are made from animal or plant tissues (such as rose madder or indigo), and inorganic dyes are made from minerals (such as cobalt or zinc). Synthetic pigments derive from the same substances as natural ones, but are produced in a lab instead of being derived from the material itself. Since synthetic dyes are much more predictable, consistent, and controllable than natural ones, they are used extensively in carpet dyeing.

It is very important to realize that the complexities of fiber production, dye construction and application and actual end use of carpet make it extremely difficult to predict any specific color's (or "hue's") performance characteristics. Any specification of carpet should include careful description of end use requirements in order for the manufacturer to ensure actual performance of the hue through pre-construction testing.

INDIGO—A deep grey/violet blue. Think Levis®.

INFRARED—An invisible light, whose wavelength is between 800 nm and 1 mm, beyond red in the visible spectrum. Although invisible to the naked eye it can be readily perceived by specially treated photographic film and images can be recorded combining visible objects and invisible infrared emissions, when shot through a suitable (usually orange) FILTER.

INTERIOR DECORATION—Danger! See INTERIOR DESIGN.

INTERIOR DESIGN—The selection, design and coordination of the interior elements of a structural space, such as a room, house, or office, including color, furniture, fittings, equipment, and even architectural detail; the person who does this is a Designer. Some Designers consider the word "Decorator" a condescending term implying merely putting ornamentation on surfaces; *don't say "Interior Decorator" unless the person of whom you are speaking uses it first.*

IVORY—Creamy, almost white.

JEWEL TONES—SATURATED, bright colors, reminiscent of sparkling gems. The colors must be clear and bright, verging on harsh; if a color is saturated but not bright, it is *intense* rather than a jewel tone.

JADE—An uncertain word, meaning a color ranging from bluish green to yellowish green, as does the stone for which it is named. The word "jaded," which derives from an obscure and unclear source in the 14th Century, means "tired or worn out; effete" which leads to a psychological back formation suggesting that "jade" implies a faded color. The term does not appear on the *Verbal Spectrum* below.

KELVIN—William Thomson, 1st Baron of Kelvin (1824-1907) was a British mathematician who developed the Kelvin (or "absolute") scale of temperature. Please see COLOR TEMPERATURE.

KHAKI—A light yellowish tan. Because of the military connotations, many people confuse khaki and OLIVE, both of which have been used for uniforms in the US Army (summer and winter, respectively). The army now uses battle camouflage in shades of green, because of the large number of 200 pound green animals found in nature.

LAVENDER—Pale bluish purple.

LEMON—A clear, bright yellow with hints of green.

LIGHT—Since HUE (or "color") is directly dependent on the presence or absence of certain frequencies in the spectrum of the light under which something is viewed (in other words, since the color of the light will affect the color of the carpet), accuracy *and consistency* of the light used when comparing samples is essential. If the carpet will be viewed under fluorescent light, samples should be matched under tubes of the same age and design as those in the final application; the same is true for product to be viewed under incandescent or day light. The MACBETH LIGHT is an industry standard of source light. See also OTT LIGHT.

LIGHT, SPEED OF—Now *here* is a concept with which to conjure! The first person to figure out how to measure the speed of light was Ole Roemer who, in 1676, came up with a reliable estimate. Over 100 different people used varying techniques until in 1983 the speed of light was established at 299,792.458 kilometers (km) per second. By obvious extension, that makes a meter the distance traveled by light in a vacuum in 1/299,792,458 seconds. Generally, the number is rounded up to a speed of 300,000 km/sec, or 186,000 miles per second.

But the story gets better. The speed of light was measured more than 163 times during the more-than-300 years from Ole Roemer to the Seventeenth General Congress on Weights and Measures in 1983. In each of these repeated experiments, it is reported that the *speed was shown to be slightly lower than that found by the previous experimenters.* (Although the Present Author has not personally verified each of those claims, he has no reason to doubt the statement.) Consider the implications: if there were nothing more than an increasing degree of specificity at work, some measurements should show light faster than previous measurements, and others show it as being slower. If it is true that each measurement shows a slightly slower speed, that could imply that light is slowing down. If that were true, that could imply that the RED SHIFT (the measurement of movement of the red band in the SPECTRUM of a distant star, showing its apparent speed of movement from the observers on Earth) is being incorrectly measured, which could demonstrate both that the universe is smaller and younger than it appears to be. This would throw almost everything known about the universe into a cocked hat. It also would do grave damage to Einstein's Theory of Relativity, since (as is well known) its simplest mathematical expression, demonstrating the relativity of everything in existence ($e=mc^2$, where "e"=energy, "m"="mass," and "c"=the speed of light) depends on the speed of light being a constant.

As you can see, historically these developments have occurred at the rate of roughly 1 measurement per 6 months, although in reality new measurements appear much more often than that these days. Keep on eye on the scientific press for new developments—especially any showing a new, slightly slower discovery of the "actual" speed of light.

LILAC—Pale reddish-purple.

LIME—Bright yellowish green.

LUSTER—The brightness or reflectiveness of fibers, yarns, carpets, or other fabrics.

MACBETH® (LIGHT)—A trade name for a standard light source under which objects can be viewed for COLOR MATCHING. See OTT LIGHT.

MARIE-THERÉSE YELLOW—See MUSTARD.

MAUVE—A pale bluish purple, much used by the artist of the same name.

METALLIC—A color that has some of the visual properties of a metal, especially that of a luster or shine deeper than that of a plastic and suggestive of physical strength and durability.

MONOCHROMATIC (COLOR SCHEME)—A color palette based on shades and tints of a single color.

MUSTARD—Yellowish-brown color; Flagler or Maria-Therése yellow approach it. Col. Mustard is a character in the thoroughly admirable family board game *CLUE®*.

NAVY—Dark, pure blue color without any purplish cast.

OCHRE—A muddy, pale orange yellow color.

OLIVE—An ocher or deep yellow green, as of the color of the unripened fruit of the olive tree.

OPAQUE—Impervious to light rays; solid, impenetrable. By logical extension the term now has come to suggest dense or insensitive.

ORANGE—The color of the fruit of the same name, pumpkins, and the royal house of the Netherlands; one of the three secondary colors, the wavelength of which is between 590 and 610 nm (nanometers), produced by blending red and yellow.

OTT (LIGHT)—A special bulb designed by Dr. John Nash Ott using rare-earth phosphors to produce artificial light that accurately reproduces daylight. This allows much more accurate evaluation of how given hues will appear in use. This is not the same as a MACBETH light, which produces an industry *standard*—rather, the purpose of an Ott Light is to make things *naturally attractive.*

OVERTONE—The appearance of a color or luster lying on top of the base color. The two primary occurrences of overtone are with lustrous or shining materials that have a hue of their own (such as METALLIC colors, or fabrics with a reflective nap, such as satin), or with colors that have been coated with a TRANSLUCENT film whose color contrasts with the base hue. Also see UNDERTONE.

PERIWINKLE—Blue-violet color.

PEWTER—A dull greyish METALLIC color usually low LUSTER, sometimes with complex undertones.

PIGMENT—A HUE-bearing particle that will not dissolve in a liquid, but which can be carried by the liquid in a solution. When the liquid is presented to another surface—such as a carpet fiber in which there is available a suitable dye site—the particle of pigment will leave the carrying liquid, bond to the dye site, and thereby impart to it the hue which it displays. Pigment particles can be differentiated by size and/or electrical conductivity as well as hue; if pigments of differing *hues* which also differ in their *size* or *electrical charge*, are placed in suspension in a given liquid, and a fabric in which fibers of *correspondingly* different dye sites have been manufactured is then immersed in the liquid, a *multi*-hued effect can be produced by a *single* dyeing. Neat stuff—(dyestuff, actually).

PUCE—Dark brownish purple color, like a flea (French *puce*, Latin *pūlic*).

PURPLE—The color of the so-called blueberries, and various flowers and shells, rather rare in nature (and hence both prized and associated with the powerful and wealthy); one of the three secondary colors, the wavelength of which is below 450 nm (nanometers), made by blending red and blue.

RED—The color of blood, stop lights, ripe tomatoes and cardinals (both birds and priests); one of the three PRIMARY COLORS, the WAVELENGTH of which is between 610 and 780 nm (nanometers).

RED SHIFT—A method of determining a light-emitting celestial body's speed of travelling as measured from another body. Since white LIGHT contains all colors, the wavelength of each component color can be measured, and if the object in question is moving relative to another object the wave lengths of each color will shift (due to the Doppler effect, the same force that lowers the pitch of a train whistle passing an observer). Comparing the wavelength of the red component of the white light to its "normal" wavelength (610 to 780) nm is using the red shift to determine relative speed.

ROSE—A term of uncertain meaning; it can refer to anything from a light crimson to a purplish or pinkish red color. To the degree that it has any meaning, the last sense—pinkish red—probably is the most useful, and it is in that sense that it is placed on the *Verbal Spectrum*.

ROYAL BLUE—A rich, SATURATED blue with a slightly reddish cast and a regal air.

SAFFRON—A color tending toward yellow-orange, like the flowers from which it originally was derived.

SATURATED/SATURATION—The intensity, depth or purity of a color or hue.

SCARLET—A bright red color, tending toward orange.

SHADE—A slight variation of color intensity within a given HUE. For Slim Shady, see Eminem; for Dante, a shade was a ghost or specter—see BIO-PLASMIC ENERGY.

SIENNA—Reddish-brown color.

SILVER—A whitish METALLIC color distinguished by being both more complex (that is, having a wider range of overtones) and by being slightly WARMER than other similar colors.

SPECTRUM—A spectrum can mean any group of things arranged in accordance with some rule or other; thus, there could be a spectrum of particles from least to greatest mass, a spectrum of politicians from least to most corrupt, or anything else. Usually (and, in this book, always) the term refers to light arranged in a straight line by wavelength or energy, as in "Red/Orange/Yellow/Green/Blue/Violet." (An easy way to remember the spectrum is to add one more color—Indigo—in its proper place and then memorizing the name "Roy G. Biv"; the letters remind you of the colors.) A spectrum can be produced by passing white light through a glass or crystal prism, whose density slows the components of light down so they are separated and projected on a surface. Finally, a shibboleth: the plural of "spectrum" properly is "spectra"; "spectrums" is a barbarism to be avoided if at all possible.

SPLIT COMPLEMENTARY (COLOR SCHEME)—A color palette based on using a color and two other colors on either side of the COMPLEMENTARY COLOR.

STEEL—A bluish-white METALLIC color, usually of high LUSTER.

SUBTRACTIVE (COLOR SYSTEM)—A PIGMENT-based way of achieving hue (color) effects, in which the PRIMARY colors cyan, yellow and magenta are mixed together to produce new hues (as blue and yellow producing green) or to produce variation on hues (as green and blue being mixed together to produce blue-green). Please also see SECONDARY and TERTIARY (colors), BROWN and ADDITIVE (COLOR SYSTEM).

TANGERINE—Deep, reddish orange color, as of the fruit.

TEMPERATURE—Please see COLOR TEMPERATURE.

TERTIARY COLORS—Colors (hues) produced by combining a PRIMARY color with its adjacent SECONDARY color on the COLOR WHEEL, named for its two constituent colors, such as "blue-green."

THÉ-AU-LAIT—"Tea with milk" (French); a gentle beige color natural to some terra-cotta buildings, or a paint of that color.

TINT—A light effect of a color, as applied by a WASH; a shade of the color of impure CHROMA, SATURATION or purity.

TRANSLUCENT—Admitting of some degree of light, but filtering it and adding or subtracting something from the light before it gets away. The most obvious example of a translucent object is a beer or wine bottle, which intentionally is TINTED to resist elements of white light that hasten spoilage of the contents. The translucent glass appears to add its own color to the white light (or, more accurately, actually absorbs and subtracts from the white light all colors but its own) so that the resulting light is the color of the translucent filter. Translucent materials can be FROSTED or PEARLESCENT, admitting reduced amounts of light without affecting its hue, as well. Lenses are not translucent, since while they distort an image they do not blur it; FILTERS, on the other hand, are.

TRANSPARENT—Offering no resistance to the passage of light of any color or hue; clear, invisible. The easiest way of distinguishing transparency from the condition of being TRANSLUCENT is that transparent substances allow visual images to pass through essentially unaltered, because they interrupt neither the color of the image nor the clarity of the light going through it. Thus, transparent glass reveals essentially what lies beyond it, while translucent glass reveals the object in a false color, blurred, or both. By extension, the term has come to suggest uncomplicated, obvious or without guile.

TRIADIC (COLOR SCHEME)—A color palette in which three hues evenly spaced around the color wheel are used together.

TURQUOISE—Dark bluish-green color.

UMBER—Dusky, earthen brown, sometimes with a reddish cast. The word derives from the root for "Shadow" or "Shade," which is important.

UNDERTONE—A base or ground hue that can be seen through a film or screen. The term also can imply a deeper meaning or intention on the part of the designer, as in having a color with psychological suggestions used in a seemingly innocuous situation; see the section on CHROMODYNAMICS AND CHROMOTHERAPY.

ULTRAVIOLET (UV)—An invisible light, whose wavelength is shorter than 4000 angstrom units, beyond purple in the visible spectrum. It is used in fabric plants to detect defects—such as SLUBS and contamination. Ultraviolet light is also used as a tool for accelerating the decay of dyestuffs to predict reliability and color stability in actual use; see FADING TESTS and the article on HUE.

THE VERBAL SPECTRUM

*Please notice the intent of these pages. If it were possible to communicate information from one sense (such as sight) to another (such as sound), one or the other sense would be essentially irrelevant. That the contrary is true—that each sense does things that others cannot—is self-evident (but also see Chapter VI, "Of Chromodynamics and Chromotherapy"). The problem of translating sensory information from one person to another is further exacerbated by the fact that individual perceptions are themselves idiosyncratic (see Chapter III—"How Color Works"). Thus, you and I might agree that "Chartreuse" is "Yellowish green," but might argue about which color on a chart really **was** "Chartreuse." That is the reason for the following lists, which group dictionary definitions of various colors into spectra as if they were color swatches. They use **words** upon which lexicographers have agreed so the Gentle Reader can translate them into **images.***

THE ESSENTIAL COLORS

TENDING TOWARD BLACK		**TENDING TOWARD WHITE**
(The absence of light)		*(Totality of light)*

INFRARED *(Invisible)*

```
                  MAGENTA          FUCHSIA
       GRAPE      SCARLET                     LILAC
BLOOD                 CRIMSON                     ROSE
          CERISE      RED        ADOBE     PINK
                  VERMILION
       HENNA                  TANGERINE
BURNT UMBER
            UMBER        ORANGE
       BURNT OCHER      SAFFRON
                OCHER                         CREAM
       GOLD         YELLOW                 CHAMPAGNE
                    LEMON
       OLIVE       LIME      CHARTREUSE    CELERY
                    GREEN                  CELADON
COBALT    TURQUOISE  BLUE-GREEN AQUA
              CERULEAN   CYAN
           NAVY       BLUE
                                   MAUVE
                  PERIWINKLE
EGGPLANT  INDIGO                  LAVENDER
                   PURPLE
       PUCE        VIOLET
```

ULTRAVIOLET *(Invisible)*

THE BROWN VISUAL SPECTRUM

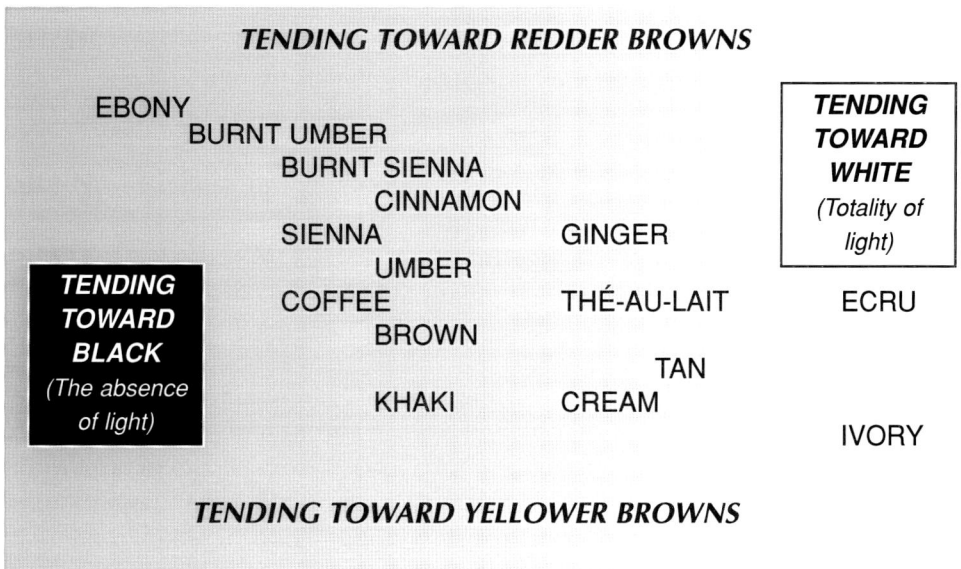

THE METALLIC COLORS

(REDDISH)
BRONZE
    COPPER
        (YELLOWISH)
        BRASS
            GOLD
                SILVER
                    (BLUISH)
                    STEEL
                        (WHITISH)
                        PEWTER
                            ALUMINUM

The Gentle Reader is lovingly reminded that the three foregoing spectra are approximate, subjective, and above all else idiosyncratic attempts by the Present Author to provide some guidelines into the words used to describe color, and that this effort (however well-intentioned) has failed once before. If you find anything here with which you disagree, please correct it (and alert the Present Author, who would be grateful).

VERMILION—A brilliant SCARLET red—rather brighter, and perhaps ever-so-slightly more yellow, than other such colors.

WAVE THEORY (LIGHT AND COLOR)—Light is not fully understood; whenever someone claims to have mastered its theory, it does something unexpected and the experts clear their throats, shuffle their feet, and change the subject. Although most people would agree that light is fundamentally an electromagnetic radiation or vibration to which eyes can react, it also
- as Einstein predicted appears to act as if it had (or at least is affected by) mass, so celestial objects can bend it;
- sometimes acts like particles (called photons), sometimes acts like *quanta* (packets of energy), and at other times it acts like a wave, and
- is distinguishable from "invisible" energy, such as *ultra* (that is, "higher than") *violet,* and *infra* (that is, "lower than") *red* only in that it has different frequencies of vibration.

Light travels from its source in all directions simultaneously, at a speed currently measured at 186,282 miles per second or 299,972 kilometers per second (although each newer, more-precise measurement reveals a slightly slower speed than the one before, suggesting that it may be slowing). White light is made up of a range of hues, or colors, each of which has its own frequency of vibration, or "wavelength"; the colors are not absolutes, but *shades* on a continuous range.

There are certain "reference points" whose wavelengths can be measured, which humans perceive in terms of response by individual receptors in the eye that sense each of the primary colors (remember, there are different primaries for pigment and light; the *eye* has receptors for blue, green, and red [the *optical* primaries] to respond to the *pigments* of blue, yellow, and red [the primary colors in pigment]. See also the entry for COLOR BLINDNESS.) The normal human eye's color receptors peak at 480 nm (cyan—a deep blue), 540 nm (green) and 600 nm (orangish-red). All receptors are quite sensitive around 570 nm which produces the perception of yellow (and are perceptive at some level to *all* the stimulating pigments).

That having been said, it becomes obvious that naming colors is a matter of gradation, rather than absolute identification. The *Verbal Spectrum,* above, is a crude attempt to place certain colors together so the names and their implications can be compared.

XENON—A gas used in a special bulb to produce an intense light by which carpet is tested for resistance to fading. Xenon also is used to produce an intense white light used by photographers attempting to approximate daylight; see COLOR TEMPERATURE.

YELLOW—The color of sunflowers, caution lights, egg yolks and lemons; one of the three PRIMARY COLORS, the WAVELENGTH of which is between 570 and 590 nm (nanometers).

CHAPTER 6
THE PSYCHOLOGIES OF COLOR

"I believe in Michael Angelo, Velasquez, and Rembrandt; in the might of design, the mystery of color, the redemption of all things by Beauty everlasting, and the message of Art that has made these hands blessed. Amen. Amen."
—George Bernard Shaw,
The Doctor's Dilemma, 1911

THE PSYCHOLOGIES OF COLOR
▲ OF CHROMODYNAMICS AND CHROMOTHERAPY ▲

INTRODUCTION AND BACKGROUND: There are many components in the visual world, such as form, motion, place, and, of course, color. It would be difficult to generalize about which of these is the most *important* in categorical terms, but almost everyone would agree that the element with the greatest *visceral* power is color. Color is the subject of chromodynamics (the study of the ability of color ["chromo"] to effect changes ["dynamics"] on "normal" environments and situations), and *chromotherapy* (the study of the ability of color to heal or support healing [therapy] in abnormal conditions). Those areas are outlined in the following essay, so that the reader will be conversant with the concepts if they should arise in a discussion with a skilled professional.

It must be noticed up front that, while both chromodynamics and chromotherapy are well-established studies at the present time, one—the area of *chromotherapy*—carries an historical burden. In the 19th Century a remarkable showman, therapist, self-proclaimed "magnetist" (some would say "charlatan") and healer named Edwin D. Babbitt coined the term, and developed a comprehensive (and lucrative) "practice" based on shining various colors of light on people with various ailments in order to cure them, with some demonstrable successes, and other failures. He and his methods have both adherents and enemies to this very day, and his books are published and studied in various countries (although his therapies cannot be used in the United States, where they have been repudiated by the medical establishment). *The following study uses his term, but does not directly draw from Babbitt's work,* because of the controversial nature of his current reputation. If you encounter an active chromotherapist (who uses the term to describe him/herself), verify quickly whence s/he comes, in order to position yourself on the right side of the "Babbitt line." That is all there is about that subject here.

Now, to the scientific bases.

THE PHYSICS AND BIOMECHANICAL PRINCIPLES: Color—or more properly, hue—depends upon light, which is an energy form of mysterious composition. Sometimes appearing to be waves, and sometimes particles, it is the source of illumination ("lighting," redundantly) for the visible world. An individual object's color is a function of its ability to absorb from the light all available wavelengths other than its own; that color, which it reflects, is what we see when we look at the object. [For more about the technical aspects of color and color theory, please see the related articles in the *Carpet and Rug Handbook*.)

The ability to see color is not shared by all living creatures, nor do all creatures see color in the same way. In fact, human beings' sense of being MIBU™ traps them: for example, is it not arrogant to assume that because *we* can see light only in the range between 380 nm (violet) and 780 nm (red), that *everyone* is limited to that range? Hasn't anyone seen *The Sixth Sense?* What is your cat looking at, anyway?

Such thoughts are important to areas as speculative as chromodynamics and chromotherapy. It is essential to keep the mind open when treading new waters, lest one mistake a treasure for a trap (or *vice versa*). That must be your guide going forward in this essay.

Historical research into the subject of the metaphysical implications of color has necessarily been limited by the ability of medical people to examine the apparatus of sight, without being able to study what happens when the information is processed in the brain; more recently, studies of brain activity with several different forms of ingenious mapping tools have extended the frontiers of knowledge—or, at least, of surmise. So, while it is known with some level of confidence that some creatures—cats and dogs, for example—lack certain mechanical structures in the eye that allow humans to see the *colors humans see,* the full implications of that issue have not been addressed.

Nor has there been study of the even more interesting question of whether each person sees the *same* color as another: that is, if you and I were to look at a stop sign and agree that the background is red, how do we know that the color that *you* call "red" is not the same one that I call "blue" or something else? In other words, we may agree on what to *call* something without actually *seeing* the same thing.

You can test part of this question very easily, in a very small way: pick an object, preferably one with a fairly neutral color (such as a medium grey panel, as the one on the facing page). Cover one eye, and examine it with the other. Memorize its color. Now open the closed eye, and cover the one that was open, and examine the same object. You will notice that one eye "sees" color slightly differently than the other (usually, one sees warmer colors, and the other cooler ones). If such a perceptible difference is possible in your *own* head, why should there not be other—and possibly even greater ones—between *your* head and *other* peoples'?

ABNORMAL AND NORMAL COLOR RESPONSES: The foregoing preambles were designed to anticipate and then avoid some obvious objections to the rest of this essay (and there are many others which could be advanced). Two must be recognized specifically: some sorts of *abnormal* psychology, and certain *parapsychological* phenomena.

For example, there is the phenomenon of synæsthesia. This is the condition in which certain people, being exposed to specific stimuli, have responses that cross normal sensory lines. Part of this is abnormal (although enviable, perhaps), and part is normal.

The abnormal application of the term refers to such things as the many synæsthetes who receive mental responses that are distinct from the normal stimuli to which they are exposed. For example, some synæsthetes perceive colors in response to certain numbers—a 5 might be red, for example, a 7 black, or a 3 blue (or anything else). These are thought not to

This neutral grey panel will be a target for your test of your eyes' individual color perception. It also is a good target for your light meter, should you still own a camera needing one.

While you are at it, you might want to determine which of your eyes is dominant—although more often than not it is the same as your dominant hand; this is not always the case. Here's how to do it: with both eyes open, look at a distant object. Now raise your hand and extend one finger so that it is aligned with that object. Then, open first one eye and then the other, in turn. With one of your eyes open, your index finger will remain superimposed on the distant object; with the other eye open, your finger will appear to spring to the right or left. The eye with which your stereo vision agrees—that is, the eye with which your finger remains in place over the object—is your dominant eye. Among other things, this determines which color message from your eyes is given preëminence in your brain's processing of conflicting data

be learned responses, but rather some unusual sensory connections in the individuals' brains. Similarly, certain feelings might evoke odors, or sounds bring up tastes. This is an important area of investigation, although not directly related to the subject at hand; therefore, those who are interested in a little more information are invited to stay with this part of the article, while those who find it too *outré* can skip ahead exactly two pages forward.

It should come as no surprise to learn that the study of synæsthesia began during the Romantic period in art history—the late 18th and early 19th Centuries, when Ludwig van Beethoven (1770-1827), Eugene Delacroix (1798-1863), and George Gordon, Lord Byron (1788-1824) (for examples) were working. This was an era in which the artist as hero, whose turmoils, anguishes and visions were perceived to be exquisite refinements of the experiences of normal people, was held up as an exemplar; these deeply-sensed sufferings of superior beings were models of the feelings to which the ordinary fold should aspire.

These were more than merely basic senses—the sensations should cross over and enrich each other. The German writer E[rnst] T[heodor] A[madeus] [Wilhelm] Hoffman [1776-1822] and—later, the French poet Charles Pierre Baudelaire (1821-1867)—expressed this; Baudelaire wrote "Scents, colors, and sounds resonate together" (*"Les parfums, les couleurs at les sons respondent"*); to him, musical tones and letters of the alphabet seemed related. To another French poet—Jean Nicolas Arthur Rimbaud (1854-1891)—various vowels sounded like certain colors. And today at least one critic—Arlene Croce—argues that Edgar Degas' (1834-1917) largely ignored painting *Portrait de Mlle E.F. ... à propos du ballet de la Source* is a specific expression of synæsthesia: it shows a horse drinking water while one woman plays a lute, another stares at her reflection in a pond while holding a flower, and a third dries her feet, suggesting the experiences of taste, sound, sight, scent, and touch, in that order. In other words, the painting is supposed to help the viewer appreciate that the art of ballet—exemplified by *Le Source,* the specific ballet in which Miss Eugénie Fiocre danced—was intrinsically a synæsthesic experience: one can hear and see the dancers (tasting, touching and smelling them are beyond the ken of the Present Author).

Some would argue that these feelings are illusions—deceptive, rather than illuminating. That illusions are powerful is inarguable; optical illusions, in particular, are easy to appreciate. On the facing page are examples of eight classic optical illusions demonstrating the power of the mind to deceive the eye. These suggest the universality of synæsthesia—that anyone can learn to understand that there is more in the visual world than is immediately obvious. Or try this: study this line:

Now go back and reëxamine the Hering illusion, on the opposite page. If now the lines seem more parallel, you are "field independent"—

SOME CLASSIC OPTICAL ILLUSIONS

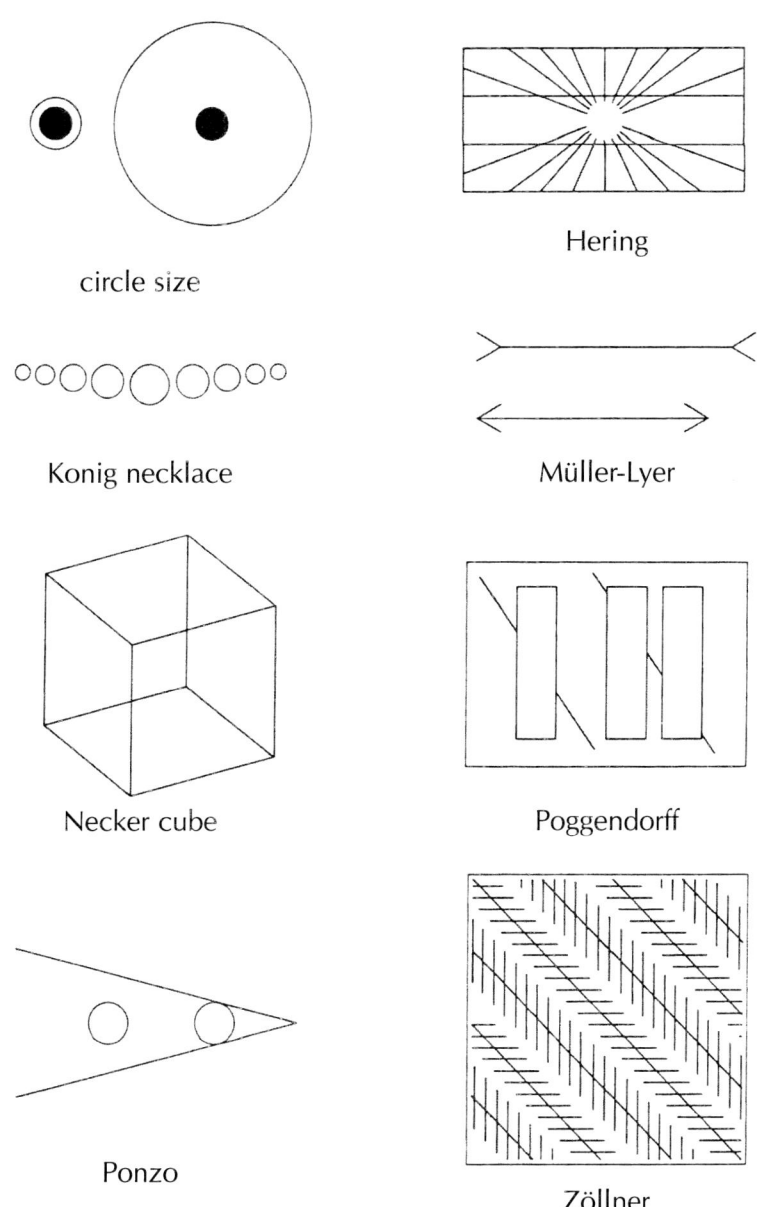

The dots in the circle size *illusion are equal size.*
The horizontal lines in the Hering *pattern are parallel.*
The tops of the circles in the Konig necklace *are on a straight line.*
Both lines in the Müller-Lyer *are equal in length.*
The Necker cube *appears to change orientation.*
The lines covered by rectangles in the Poggendorff *illusion are straight.*
The circles in the Ponzo *illusion (not to be confused with a Ponzi scheme) are equal size.*
All the diagonal lines in the Zöllner *pattern are parallel.*

more able to "compartmentalize" experiences, like President Bill Clinton; if the lines still seem curved you are more "field dependent" and synæsthesic; like President Ronald Reagan, you "see" things as part of an organic whole. That is one small example of the power of synæsthesia—the ability to combine experiences into schematic wholes. But that is the end of the subject here.

Another unusual phenomenon is the perception of *auras.* Certain people appear to have the ability to detect colored halos or auras emanating from other people, and these auras have different colors depending upon what the person is doing. These are not dependent on close study, or even being in the same room; one well-known case involved a mother and son who perceived auras; the son walked into the living room as the mother was watching a Presidential news conference, glanced casually at the screen, and asked his mother, "Hey, why is the President lying?" This aspect of color perception, while very interesting, also is not part of the present essay. (See BIOPLASMIC ENERGY in the main dictionary.)

Synæsthesia has a much more common—and very important—application, however. That lies in the ability of color to alter perceptions in most people. For example, objects painted in certain colors appear larger than the same objects in other colors; in other words, the color influences the perception of volume and/or weight. (A brilliant example of this was in the early Volkswagen Beetles. They were extremely lightweight cars, but they were painted in very dense, rich colors, which made them appear to be far more substantial than they were).

Another example lies in a color's ability to influence apparent temperature: "warm" colors (oranges and yellows, for example) tend to make a room *feel* warm, and "cool" colors (blues and certain blue-greens) make people feel cool. In one test, people felt that a temperature of 59° F was cold in a blue-green room, but were comfortable until the temperature fell to 52° F in a red-orange one; in another study, people in a light-blue cafeteria complained of being cold when the thermostat was set at 75° F; when the room was repainted orange, the setting had to be reduced to 72° F because 75° F now felt too hot.

Colors even have the ability to influence the perception of *sound.* Rooms can be made to appear more acoustically active when its walls and fixtures are yellow or red; a noisy room can be calmed, and the overall perception of noise muted, if it is fitted with darker browns, blues, and greens.

From this point forward, we should like to consider neither the likelihood of *differences* in vision and human response to color, nor the extraordinary abilities of certain people, but rather—having acknowledged that such differences and extra sensory abilities may exist—speak to those things that are *common* in human experience in responding to color. And there are lots of them.

FACTORS AFFECTING COLOR RESPONSE: Right up front, one important distinction should be drawn between the types of *design and color* used in a

A simple test of color value asks, "The manufacturer has installed different add-on packages on these cars, ranging from 'bare-bones' to 'luxury' costs. Which of these cars do you guess has the most elaborate options, and is the most expensive?" [For answers as to how your response compares to the standard, please get in touch with the author.]

space based upon its *function,* the personalities of the *people* who will use the space, and the changing *circumstances* that the people may feel as they work.

The *people* may be considered in the Jungian sense of being extraverted (channeling their energy to the external, physical world) or introverted (exploring and analyzing the internal world and its affairs). This is to be understood as part of their *Gestalt,* or entirety of existence.

The *space* may be considered by its function, as a library, kitchen, sleeping space, or whatever. This is to be understood as its *Weltanschauung*, or comprehensive place in the plane of existence.

The *circumstances* may be considered in terms of the peoples' specific condition. That is, the workload may be intense, or relaxed; the people may be mentally healthy, or mentally unhealthy, and so on. In its simplest terms, then, the outline goes as follows:

Under *normal* circumstances, people like surroundings that *match* their personality styles (whether extraverted or introverted). However, under *extraordinary* circumstances, they respond best when the environment *compensates* for their styles. In other words, an extraverted person likes an extraverted environment, unless s/he is under stress, in which case an introverted environment works more effectively.

The *space* should reflect the normal demands under which it is used, unless the *circumstances* change. In other words, a hospital surgery usually is green to calm the medical people's feelings; however, if the room were used for triage, a stronger color would be better.

The following essay accepts all the foregoing, but does not pretend to address all its issues. Study in these areas has been undertaken for years. Chief among the modern scholars are people such as Raymond Loewy, Johannes Itten, Frank Mahnke, Luigina De Grandis, and the estimable Faber Birren, among many others; the following is indebted to these, and many more.

And remember that this study is not an academic one: the business of interior décor in all its aspects is fundamentally a *business* of color, and failure to master its intricacies can lead to failures which, even though they appear to be inexplicable, are nonetheless tragic. Or, to put a more positive light on it, as Loewy wrote, "Good design" [which includes good color, of course] "keeps the user happy, the manufacturer in the black, and the æsthete unoffended."

PRACTICAL APPLICATIONS OF THE PRINCIPLES IN THE WORLD IN GENERAL: The earliest work with the subject of chromodynamics was undertaken with a practical end. The problem was the military machine working to advance the aims of the western nations during the world war that occupied most of the 20th Century; making things, making enough things, and making things that worked, were the practical aims that stoked the inventive fires of that era. Making things beautiful, or that made people feel good about themselves, or had real permanent value, were not issues

Examples of the effect of complementary color schemes used to achieve subliminal statements. What does each suggest to you about the institution so identified?

Above are logos of actual companies, past and present. Based on this Chapter, what messages do you think the psychometric specialists at the firms are sending? How do you respond to each—which of these companies project an image that you like? More about that follows!

What is the psychological message of this National Flag—again, in complementary colors?

for most of that period, so æsthetic concerns did not leap to the forefront of designers' minds.

However, failures in productivity *did* get attention; in one celebrated case, it was observed that as new, standardized office systems were sent around the world in the 1940's, error rates began to go up. Careful studies revealed that the grey metal desks, with dark grey rubberized work surfaces, that were being shipped wherever American government-issue employees were at work, were the cause, because their color was uninspiring and dispiriting, as well as providing overly stark contrast for the papers being processed. Green surfaces corrected the problem. (This was about the same time as America's classrooms were being converted from blackboards with white chalk to greenboards with yellow chalk—both for visibility, and for other reasons, outlined below).

And from this sort of observation grew the studies of chromodynamics and chromotherapy. Combinations of design and psychology, they have greatly improved the *science* of interior decoration, while reinforcing many of its insightful *intuitions.*

Of course, like all psychological considerations, the study of color gets caught on the old "nature versus nurture" debate. It isn't possible to say whether, or to what degree, people have specific color responses based on their training and societal expectations, on some form of "hard wiring" in the brain, or a combination of these two—perhaps, most intriguingly, a "hard wiring" that leads various societies to make the same selections that lead to similar nurturing of their infants.

In the case of color, there is ample evidence to support both sides: for example, the color white has exactly opposite meanings in Asian and European cultures, where it symbolizes mourning and purity, respectively. Or are those meanings so far apart? Do they share a common, hard-wired root desire for completeness and wholeness?

In the same way, when a researcher tested color responses to the word "happy" in European and American subjects, he found that green was chosen by 24% of the Europeans, and none of the Americans, while orange—its opposite (complement) was chosen with great uniformity. Here are people with very similar cultural backgrounds, selecting very different colors a significant minority of the time. Again, is this nature or nurture?

One last example—some years ago, the present author was involved in focus group testing of possible colors for a carpet line. Samplings had been drawn from several communities in the United States; one was in Birmingham, Alabama. Two test groups had been assembled; one group, shown the colors, indicated a clear preference for the brighter tones being proposed, while the other showed equal preference for the more muted shades in the line. The researcher, perplexed, mused aloud about the problem, whereupon one of the participants asked how the groups had been selected. The tester replied that postal ZIP codes had been used. The respondent smiled and explained that explained everything. Birmingham is in a "bowl" valley between two mountain ranges; one ZIP code was on the western face of the bowl, and received subdued morning sunlight in their homes, and the other was on the west-facing eastern side, and therefore got the strong afternoon sun—thus preferring the quieter colors. Neither nature *nor* nurture—merely *experience* was at work.

This issue also "illuminates" another factor: the *character and quality* of the **light** used in spaces where people live and work is no less vital than the quality of the air they breathe. There is powerful evidence that the absence of a full spectrum of light causes discomfort and even illness; one such condition—the result of living under artificial light during prolonged winter conditions, leading to depression that can be life-threatening—is called *Seasonal Affective Disorder*, or SAD. And don't forget (as noted above) that *similar* conditions can cause *different* outputs for *different* people, based on their *particular* conditions. For example there is evidence (hotly denied by the people who make light bulbs) that fluorescent lights (such as are used in most schools) cause the production of brain chemicals linked to Attention Deficit Disorder in people with a propensity for the condition. In other words, the dynamic effects of chroma can extend into the private lives (and medicine cabinets of people in many walks of life)—the ADD sufferers get dosed with Ritalin, Prozac, or similar Soma-like drugs. But, again, these are areas of *abnormal* psychology, and our focus here must be on the *mass* of human experience.

PREDICTABLE RESPONSES TO VARIOUS COLORS: What are some reasonable responses of normal people to typical colors? Happily, that is a fairly easy question to answer. In one test, Frank Mahnke gave words to subjects in both Europe and the United States and asked them to pick the colors that matched the words; although there were individual variations, of course, the following general patterns emerged:

Love	Red and red-violet
Hatred	Black (and red, in Europe)
Peace/tranquility	Blue, green, and blue-green
Mourning/sorrow	Black, grey
Happy	Yellow, orange
Disease/caution	Yellow
Jovial	Orange, yellow
Life	Green (Europeans also picked red)
Luminous	Yellow, yellow-orange
Noble	Blue, violet, blue and red violet

However, these general preferences are inadequate for space planning because, as noted above (and as is immediately obvious to any reader), there also are differences in response based on *individual* situations, and those individual responses are further modified by *specific and particular circumstances.* Here, the work of Johannes Itten and, especially, Faber Birren, kick in, and offer important support. Taking *colors* as the starting point and working back toward *attitudes* within the context of *individuals,* numerous studies have shown people colors and then determined what their reactions were. Again, there is a great deal of useful unanimity, with individual *variation*. Some generalizations include the following:

Red—is one of the two most universally preferred colors (the other is blue). It is arousing (it can even raise blood pressure); stimulating, and aggressive; often used for combat signals (and was even used for battle uniforms in former times). It is the color of blood, and of romance. Add white and it becomes pink, and assumes feminine versions of these attributes.

People who like red tend to be extraverted, either naturally or by choice. Those who come to it naturally are impulsive, outspoken, and extreme in their emotions; if carried to an extreme, these people can be bipolar or even manic-depressive. Those who *force* themselves to choose this color are fundamentally timid, and wish to change; they tend to wish-fulfillment and often are over-achievers.

For example, it has been the experience of the Present Author that men who choose to join the United States Marine Corps (an organization long associated with its bright red uniforms) tend to be either willful and extreme people who love adventure and danger, or reflective, sensitive people who choose this avenue as a way of testing and satisfying themselves. These are the people of the color red.

People who dislike red tend to be frustrated, bitter, and angry.

Orange—has few *cultural* associations; until it becomes dense, when it becomes overpowering. Psychologically, it is a friendly, associative color, suitable for pubs and bars. When *darkened* it becomes brown, which is a nurturing, comforting, dulling, enveloping color. Brown was the color of peasants in the medieval period.

People who like orange tend to be gregarious and agreeable. Faber Birren claims that people who like orange tend to remain unmarried. People who dislike orange tend to be moralistic, almost gloomy sorts; often they dislike salespeople. Be forewarned.

People who like brown are simple, sturdy, and shrewd. It also is preferred by the mentally troubled. People who dislike brown are easier to understand: they tend to be open and enthusiastic.

Yellow—suggests activity, enthusiasm, happiness, and daylight, although it also can be associated with caution or disease. For most people, however, it has a long-recognized power to stimulate shoppers, in part because it inspires hope and suggests the sun. There is lots of yellow on the shelves of a variety store, and relatively little in the grocery—until you get to the cleaning products, pet food, and snacks. Yellow's muted orange cousin, saffron, is associated with wisdom and even holiness.

People who like yellow are at the extremes of the intelligence spectrum: they either are very bright, or retarded. Solipsists in particular like the color, and so did the fictional character Nero Wolfe (see the magnificent series of novels by Rex Stout)—who was both a genius and an egoist, if not a solipsist. Since intelligent people are better able than most to predict the consequences of actions, and shy away from actions whose consequences are undesirable, the color has come to be associated with cowardice.

Here are four logos for a business. Each sends a different message. Please ask yourself the following questions:
- Which of these would be the best logo for a fast-food restaurant?
- Which would be the best logo for a high-end restaurant?
- Which would be the best for an investment firm?
- Which would you trust least?

To discover how your reactions compare to the test groups, please get in touch with the Present Author. Or, simply reflect on them, and get in touch with yourself!

People who dislike yellow tend to be anti-intellectual or disliking of cowards. The Magen David imposed on Jews in Germany during the era of National Socialism (Nazism) was yellow, for any of a number of obvious possible reasons. Since people tend to reject most strongly the weaknesses they most fear in themselves, the dislike of yellow may merely reflect a fear of being stupid—based on self-awareness—or a fear of contamination.

Green—relaxes, rests, and suggests growth and renewal. Birren calls it "The most American of colors." It is excellent for places where people need to be set at ease. It can lower blood pressure, and is used in hospital operating rooms to calm the physicians (for which, thank goodness). Green was the color of Muhammad's cloak, and is the traditional color for brides in Palestine. Overdone, green gets negative connotations; it has a place, and should not leave it. If you want to scare someone at Hallowe'en, shine a green light upward from your chin on your face. Everything is wrong, and everyone knows it.

People who like green appreciate the good life; they often are well-mannered, even-tempered, sophisticated, and overweight. People who dislike green often are mentally unstable, lonely, and highly intellectual (and bitter about it). The present author has no data upon which to base this, but would not be surprised to learn that the Unabomber disliked green (and Kermit the Frog).

Blue/green (aqua, turquoise, chartreuse, et alii)—This is a strange one. Notice the various names for shades of this color: words drawn from the sea, stones, and strange beverages. This is a complicated color, with complicated responses. It suggests peace and tranquility, and can be used to great effect in medical environments (see below)—but the people who *like* it tell a different story. They tend to be discriminating, refined, sophisticated, and charming. However, Birren's research shows they also tend to be artificial, fussy, vain, self-centered, and very much more nasty stuff that won't be discussed here. (His research also indicates that people who like blue-green tend to be divorced—there's something to take to your marriage counselor).

Things are scarcely better among those who dislike blue-green. While they dislike conceit or pretension in others, it is because of their own self-centered arrogance: their *personal* confidence makes them dislike the confidence of other people. If you have strong feelings about blue-green, you might want to readjust yourself. Or find people like you. See MIBU™.

Blue—is one of the two most commonly preferred colors (the other is red). It has few enemies. It is the color of thought, conservatism, dedication to work, and achievement. In Rome it was the color of philosopher's robes, and still suggests wisdom. Blue is the color of holiness in Judaism; Krishna is blue in Hinduism. Yet it also suggests sorrow (as in "the blues"). A blue environment makes people feel at ease, more comfortable, and contemplative. Blue is the color of both the sky and the (idealized) sea, and therefore suggests travel and open spaces.

People who like blue tend to be affiliative (they seek out people like themselves), which makes them reliable. They tend to be conservative,

In a recent election in a politically conservative State, Republican and Democrat candidates ran for various state and local offices. These photographs—from the windows of their respective campaign headquarters—show the difference between the political philosophies of the parties, as expressed by their color choice. The Republicans, as you can see, mostly chose red, white, and blue; yellow and green dominated for the Democrats. (Incidentally, the Republicans swept all but a few offices—can you guess which Republicans and Democrats lost on the basis of these colors? You'd probably be right.)

or even reactionary. They are steady, responsible, and positive. People who like *dark* blue are extreme examples of the type.

People who *dislike* blue are guilty, revolutionary, resentful about others' accomplishments, or merely worn out after striving and achieving less than they feel they deserve.

In short, any reasonable person will not be surprised by the fact that George Bush, Ronald Reagan, and other Republicans have campaigned under a blue banner, while John McCain, Ted Kennedy, and Hilary Clinton favor green (or yellow). Surprise, surprise! (as Gomer Pyle, USMC, might say).

Purple—has for so long been associated with royalty (because of the scarcity and cost of the shellfish from which it was made, in ancient Rome) that it cannot be considered independent of its cultural associations. It suggests nobility, and is worn for solemn occasions (such as Lent) in Christian churches. Magicians also tend toward the color. In other words, the associations of purple are "otherworldly," in many ways.

People who like purple tend to be artistic, ethereal, creative, or exotic, or tend to want to be perceived as those things. Whether they *are* what they *appear* to be, or merely *strive* to appear to be what they appear to be, is more important to their therapists than to their suppliers. Respond to them as they desire, because, for them form matters.

People who dislike the color purple, on the other hand, tend to be outspoken tigers, and the person who wishes to work with them must make a careful effort to learn precisely where they are. Enemies of purple dislike pretense, conceit, and artifice; often, they are anti-intellectual, and perceive people who value the life of the mind as being phonies. They can be very dangerous to the fashion-oriented professional.

White—symbolizes hope and purity in the West, and death in the East. It is the absence of color, and thus symbolizes the absence of other things—sin, corruption, or life. Almost no one selects it as a favorite "color" (except for schizophrenics—be afraid—be very afraid!)

Black—suggests the power of darkness, power, and authority. Priests' cassocks, rabbis' suits, fearsome military people of all sorts, teenagers, the President's Secret Service (America's own SS)—all wear black. Black is also the color of the "authoritarian servant"—the musicians in the orchestra, for example, or the headwaiter in a fine restaurant. Since black makes accessories look good, it also is the choice for evening wear. It does not make for a good wall color.

Grey is a mixture of black and white. Since the associations of the two hues are opposites, the end result is nothing: grey, in other words. Preference for grey almost always is a conscious, deliberate choice, and therefore something to be evaluated carefully.

TYPICAL AMERICAN COLOR SYMBOLISM: In the preceding sections of this essay/article, we have been at pains to acknowledge and honor the fact that different cultures have developed different responses to specific colors.

At the same time, we have been at equal pains throughout the whole of this little Book to make its content relevant to the professional communicator practicing in the United States in the 21st Century. In this section, we therefore shift from a global approach to a purely local one, and investigate some of the responses to specific colors that work in the United States at this time.

Notice the words "at this time" at the end of the last paragraph. Any effort to identify responses to anything as powerful as color must recognize that there are both *biomechanical* components in the response mechanisms (that is, responses that may be "hard-wired" in the brain, for more information about which please see the next section) and *conditioned responses*— things "learned" and stored in the more temporal (that is, "time-based") areas of the brain. Thus, if you were abducted by aliens who placed you in a terrarium on their spaceship, and the walls of your terrarium were painted bright purple, your response to the color purple would forever be altered by your experiences while a captive. The *type* of your response would be conditioned by what happened; if, in the terrarium, you were treated with attentiveness and learned to love your captors, you would have one set of associations to the color; if they tortured you, your associations would be different.

With that *caveat,* let us consider the symbolism of basic colors in the United States at the present time. Much of the information in this section grows naturally from or even duplicates the previous one; the information is offered here in simple tabular form for easier reference.

Red—Symbolizes warmth, energy, power, excitement, strength, love, sexual relationships, and dominance.

Orange—Energy, warmth, cheer, good times, excitement, activity; it has a tinge of aggressiveness and assertiveness as well.

Yellow—Cheer, hope, communication, optimism, egotism, communication, encouragement, health, vitality—but also decay and caution.

Green—Nature, growth, sustenance, freshness, renewal, hope, youth, envy, peace, good luck, physical coolness.

Blue—Masculinity, spirituality, understanding, trust, technology, security, truth, cleanliness, tranquility, withdrawal, physical coldness.

Purple—Magic, mystery, spirituality, faith, dignity, creativity, passion, awareness; a hint of regality clings to it—even this egalitarian culture— as well.

Brown—Hominess, soothing, nature, durability, dullness, realism, warmth, security, reliability, and comfort.

White—Newness, cleanliness, sterility, purity, innocence, chastity, spirituality, refinement, and truth.

Black—Power, complexity, sophistication, the unknown, death and emptiness.

Grey—Neutrality, intelligence, modesty, technology, security, tranquility, coldness, withdrawal and retirement.

Multiple colors send multiple or multi-layered messages, obviously; black and red together—the colors of the German National Socialists— speak loudly about attitudes, just as do the blue and white of the Israeli flag.

The red-white-and-blue of the United States, the Netherlands, England France, and several other countries send psychological messages of energy, reliability, and truth that most of us wish other people would believe a little more enthusiastically.

And multiple colors provide another good example of the changeability of the message sent by colors. When the present author's son moved into a new bedroom 30 years ago, we placed a rainbow sticker on the window over his bed as a symbol of hope and promise. 20 years later, the rainbow had become the symbol of The Walk to Emmaus, a Christian lay organization. Today, of course, the rainbow has become a symbol of gay and lesbian pride. The window didn't change, but the message it sent most assuredly did. For this reason, all the information in this section of this essay—since it is intentionally based on practice in a specific country (the United States) at a specific time (the first decade of the 21st Century)—must be regarded as flexible at best, and untrustworthy without confirmation at worst.

Nonetheless, now that you are armed with this knowledge, it would be an entertaining exercise to examine the logos and other symbols of various businesses to determine the messages they are sending to customers. In most cases, these messages are far from accidental; the people who design business symbols are very highly-paid professionals who use complex models and sophisticated polling techniques to send messages with laser-like precision. On the other hand, some companies have accidental messages—these are the fun ones to find and giggle about.

TYPICAL BIOMECHANICAL RESPONSES TO COLORS: In addition to the *symbolisms* of colors as explored in the preceding sections, there also are *physical reactions* to colors—biomechanical responses that matter to the designers and users of spaces. Some are very important in the *use* of a space, as in deciding what color to paint its walls and ceilings; for more about that, please see the following section. Others are equally important in a different way they can change the perception *of the room itself*. That is the subject of this section.

For the purposes of the color practitioner, there are only eight hues to worry about—black is unlikely to appear on the walls or ceilings of a space, except for such specialized areas as darkrooms, magician's stage sets, Goth night clubs, or spook houses at Hallowe'en (or in the rooms of teenage boys, but that's an area we absolutely will not explore). The other hues, and the normal biomechanical responses to them, are as follows:

Red—This aggressive color advances toward the viewer, producing the impression that objects are closer than they are. Red can make a room feel smaller than it "really" is, which is good if it is a very large room. Obviously, it also will make the room appear to be warmer than it is, and can make it appear to be noisier. Red strains the eye; on the other hand, pink—its paler sibling—relaxes the eye and brain.

Orange—As you would expect, orange shares characteristics of its component colors, red and yellow. However, while it does a great job of making people feel warm, it tends to *subdue* the perception of sound. Bright oranges advance toward the eye as well as reds, and are perceived almost as well as yellows; dull oranges—browns—are almost inconspicuous. The eye does not respond vigorously to them, in other words, which is another way of saying there is less biomechanical response.

Yellow—This is the color the human eye processes first—mechanically, in other words, if a spectrum is presented to the eye this is the one that registers before the others. The eye requires the most energy to process yellow, as well, and therefore it can be a fatiguing color. Since the eye processes yellow first, it should come as no surprise that it is also the most visible and luminous color to the human eye. This leads to a brief digression: many years ago, "Stop" signs in the United States were yellow with black lettering, which was much better from a safety standpoint than the current white-on-red for two reasons: first, the most common form of COLOR BLINDNESS in the world is red/green Daltonism, so that to a person with that condition a red stop sign essentially disappears against a green tree; second, red registers as a color nanoseconds after yellow does, with the result that a yellow stop sign will get a reaction sooner than a red one. Continuing this digression even further, many years ago there was no required standardized color for school busses, and various states chose various combinations—North Carolina, for example, used a really funky orange that always spooked people driving from New York to Florida. Yellow was chosen as the standardized color for school busses for precisely this same reason: almost every driver can see it, and see it quickly. Yellow's implication of *caution* probably also affected the decision.

One last digression—many gentle woodland creatures are totally insensitive to the red-orange-yellow colors, making the so-called "blaze" camouflage worn by hunters a terrific safety tool. The colors perceived as vigorous and assertive by humans are invisible to their prey.

Green—This color requires less energy to process than the others, and is perceived as being restful; in fact, it can almost fade in the background in certain situations—the field uniforms of the United States Army in the Second Part of the World War were olive drab (a deep, dull brownish-green), and currently are a purer dark green; the field uniforms of the German *Wehrmacht* were "Field grey"—a dull, deep greyish green. Both of these (adversarial) groups were striving for the same thing: inconspicuousness. This calming, low-energy near-invisibility led Faber Birren to conclude that a pale grey-green was the worst possible color for dangerous environments, such as Physical Plants in institutions—which, no doubt, is why there is a particular shade of pastel green known commercially as "P-Plant Green." This is not the whole story, of course; there are many variations of green, each with its own character. For example, chartreuse shares hues and traits with yellow, and aqua shares hues and traits with blue. Therefore, whether a particular green will recede or advance, be seen swiftly or slowly, use little energy or much energy, and so on, depends on the specific green being discussed. A little extrapolation goes a long way with a color as ubiquitous as green.

Blue—This color recedes from the eye, giving the impression that objects are farther away than they are. Even dark blues tend to be calming, which is a surprise. *Trompe l'oeil* decors in European castles and ecclesiastical residences often make much of the interplay between blue's tendency to recede and red's tendency to advance. Even the cobalt blues tend to be make a room appear to be cooler than it is, and subdue sounds in the space; the cooler cerulean blues do an even better job of this, of course.

Purple—The eye has a very difficult time dealing with purple, perhaps precisely because it is composed of one color that recedes and is cool, and one that advances and is warm. It tends to make things indistinct, and lends a sense of insecurity—even in its lighter, lilac tones.

Brown—See orange, above.

White—Pure white causes glare and forces stark contrasts. Biomechanically, this is a bummer; the resulting eyestrain is very unpleasant for most people. White should be used as an accent, therefore, rather than as something to slather over a wall or ceiling, unless the space is to be used in low light.

Grey—This is the simplest color for the eye to see—easier, even, than green. It neither stimulates nor subdues any emotions, sends no messages of noise or temperature, and—in short—just lies there. Grey makes an excellent color when visual perspicuity over an extended period of time is required but lousy when attention to detail is needed; in places where people need to be attentive to the possibility of danger, it is a terrible choice. The "P-Plant Green" mentioned above is, obviously, a greyish green, adding insult to injury (in many cases, literally).

These summaries are intended as *guidelines;* for some possible *applications,* please see the next section.

THE APPLICATION OF SPECIFIC COLORS TO SPECIFIC WORKSPACES:

The foregoing leads to some generalities about the "right" colors for various spaces. Notice, however, that the quotation marks around the word "right" are there to remind us that these are *merely* generalities; the specifics—of case, of place, of persons, of intents, and so on—may make any of the following false. Notice also that these are the most superficial of observations: a true color professional will have her or his own ideas and theories, for which the following is merely an introduction.

With that having been accepted, here are the *mere generalities.*

Offices: Both productivity and harmony are required in these areas. Therefore, the colors will need to be carefully chosen. Cool hues will aid concentration; yellows, pale golds, pale greens, and tans will always be suitable. Avoid colors that provoke strong responses, such as vivid shades of any hue, red, purple and violet, greens, reds, and the deadly white or grey. Deep blues, in particular, tend to erode enthusiasm and reduce productivity.

Health care: There are many spaces in a health care facility, each with its own requirements. Corridors should be comforting, as should waiting areas; pale hues should dominate. Patient rooms should be soothing as

If you wonder about the power of color, and the importance of selecting the right tones for a specific application, let this final, silly example serve as a touchstone. Which would you recommend for a hunter's den or study? Which for the bride's room at a wedding chapel?

well, and again pale green, aqua, pale oranges or sandstone would be good. Ceilings can be tinted (because patients stare at them a lot), and the ends of the rooms with headboards should *not* be tinted, so as not to mislead the eye of the attending physicians. Operating rooms typically are green or blue-green, which should be continued. There is great research in the area of hospital spaces (which will not be repeated here), down to specifics for recovery rooms, cancer wards, treatment rooms, and even specific areas used for specific diagnostic devices (such as electrocardiograms and roentgenology).

Industrial environments: Again, there is a range of possibilities; factors to consider include the noise level, ambient temperature (and desired perceived temperature), odors, and functions of the spaces. Obviously, an area used for color matching would have different requirements than one used for high-speed product assembly with dangerous machinery. In general, ceilings should be white or off-white, rhythmic color patterns matching workflow are appropriate, moving equipment should be bright yellow, and the colors should complement any natural hues of the material being processed.

Schools: Should be much the same as offices; beige, pale green, and blue green are good general tones, as are light yellows. The wall faced by students in a class should be a different color from the others. A study by Dr. Harry Wohlfarth in the early 1980's is instructive for those dealing with specialists in this area, to which the Gentle Reader is respectfully referred. Along the way, it is instructive to consider the complexities of the task: the space must be stimulating, but not too stimulating, encouraging of conversation, but not noisy, and bright, but not overbearing.

In this regard, please refer back to the article on light in this book, and to the discussion of acoustics in *Shibboleths and Shorthand.*

Entertainment: Two types of venue require two types of coloration, and both are greatly affected by the acoustics of the space. Most non-athletic auditoriums (movie theaters, concert halls, and the like) strive for a sense of dignity, tradition, and even solemnity; thus, deep colors and wood tones predominate. Maroon is almost always present; forest greens may be massing like Ents and preparing a return as well. In athletic settings, the energy levels are higher, and consequently the colors are more intense; unless the logo of a particular team (pro or con) has an effect, red is common.

Ecclesiastical: The subject of the significance of color to specific worship spaces is too demanding—and too specialized—for this little book. And the individual situations have powerful influence as well. So, the new Cathedral of Our Lady of the Angels in Los Angeles is almost entirely in pale beiges; the Cathedral of Saint Paul in Saint Paul is a rainbow of gold and colors set into granite architecture, and your local church, mosque, temple, cathedral, synagogue, chapel, oratory, basilica, shrine, ashram, or tabernacle could be anything from red to purple. This subject, obviously, cuts to the heart of color symbolism more than any other, because faith drives decisions with greater urgency than anything else—witness the wars of the past, present, and possible future. As you consider the colors suitable for a religious space, it is more important than anywhere else to start with what its *purpose* will be (celebration, contemplation, instruction, inspiration, and so on), what its *theology* values (redemption, confession, submission, and so on) and what its *practitioners* wish to demonstrate (wealth, charity, modernity, tradition, and so on). Then a color palette can emerge, and a scheme from that. But never forget that beneath it all lurks a veiled symbolic language unique to the faith: no green on the floor of a mosque, blue to signify the Virgin Mary, and so on.

Hospitality: There are too many variations in this industry to make any useful generalizations—a comparison of Jack-in-the-Box and its customers to a Ruth's Chris Steak House will show why. Generally, apply the rules in this Appendix with good common sense and you'll do fine in a conversation with a color specialist working in an hospitality environment.

Retail environments: Shops and stores need to stimulate people to action, so yellows (especially warm golds) almost always are a good choice. However, other factors enter in, chief among them being the type of merchandise being sold and the desired psychological impact on the customer. Thus, white is suitable for pseudo-health care (such as an optical shop), or pink is appropriate for intimate apparel (think Victoria's Secret®). Again, the *general* rules outlined in this appendix should be applied to the *specific* environment.

In this context, the Present Author is reminded of a personal experience. Some years ago he designed a retail stereo and CD store, coloring the interior a bright, light yellow. The owner had a minority partner who complained that no record stores were yellow; they were all red and black. After some weeks of steady pressure, the owner reluctantly agreed and repainted the store's walls light grey with red and black accents. Sales immediately fell 20% and stayed that way for two weeks. Alarmed, the owner had the walls repainted a yellow even stronger than the first one. Sales zoomed up to 5% *higher than the original.* The store stayed yellow for 20 years. Recently, the owner decided to relocate; the new store he proudly confided, will be even brighter yellow than the old one.

FURTHER RESOURCES: Of course, these brief paragraphs merely scratch the surface; there is far more to say about color, its implications, and its consequences, than there is room for here. For the interested professional, there are many books to read that will advance a career, which are listed under the heading *Vade Mecum* at the front of this book. Of them, the most immediately relevant is Frank Mahnke's *Color, Environment, and Human Response* (John Wiley, New York, 1996).

This is a fascinating study. The present author wishes you well in it.

"I long for the day when a human is judged by the color of his or her character rather than the color of his or her skin."
—Martin Luther King (alt)

APPENDIX

"My spelling is Wobbly. It's good spelling but it Wobbles, and letters get in the wrong places."
—Winnie-the-Pooh
(A[lan] A[lexander] Milne

APPENDIX

We *(That is, the Present Author and his Friends and Relations)* hope that you have both enjoyed and benefited from this little book. We have tried to open for you some of the principles of color and the way it is used in the worlds of Interior Design and Architecture; we hope that the fact that you are reading these words implies that you enjoyed the process at least enough to stay with it to this point. But did it actually help you? Do you feel that you now are better able to study the world around you? And, more important, are you now likely to be more comfortable and confident when working with true professionals in the field?

To discover the answers to these last questions, the following Appendix is offered as a sort of personal "show and tell" for your own use.

Herewith are line drawings of a room scene, like the ones used earlier in this book. It is generic, as you can see, consisting of a counter, two walls, a floor, a rack or shelf of some kind (to the left of the counter) and a wall or storage area behind the counter:

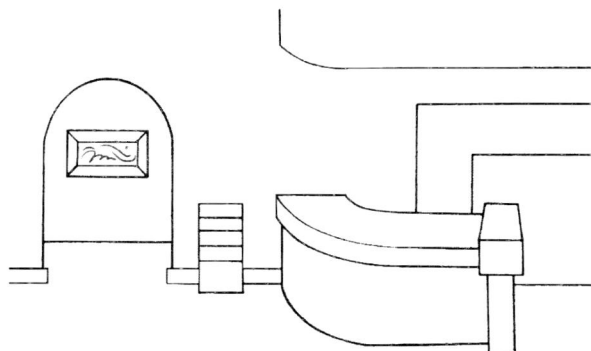

This lends itself to many practical applications; six possibilities follow as six scenarios. They differ in the application or use of the space, which therefore changes the way it should be colored to meet specific needs. Your mission, should you choose to accept it, is to design a color scheme for each space. Hopefully, that will be fun as well as revealing for you.

There are neither right nor wrong answers to these scenarios, of course, since each is a matter of impression, interpretation, and application of the principles in this book. However, if you would like to discover how some real-world professional interior designers solved these problems, please email, call, fax or write us *(the Present Author and his Friends and Relations, remember?)* at the address in the front of this book, and you'll receive the designers' color plans. As usual, the Secretary (the person who handles the mail) will disavow any knowledge of your actions. Good luck!

SCENARIO 1:
The reception/sign-in area in a high-end restaurant

Situation: *Place Piglet,* a European-style dining establishment where the average per-person ticket is over $75.00 plus drinks and tips, wants to set the appropriate tone when people approach the waiting area of the *maître (maîtresse)-d'hôtel.* The arch at left leads into the restaurant proper, into which s/he will guide the guests when good and ready; the rack to the left of the counter contains menus, which the restaurant wants people to read (to avoid sticker shock when they are seated). Please color this space for them. (In this and all following exercises, remember that you can use *hues, tints,* and *shades* in various types of combination.)

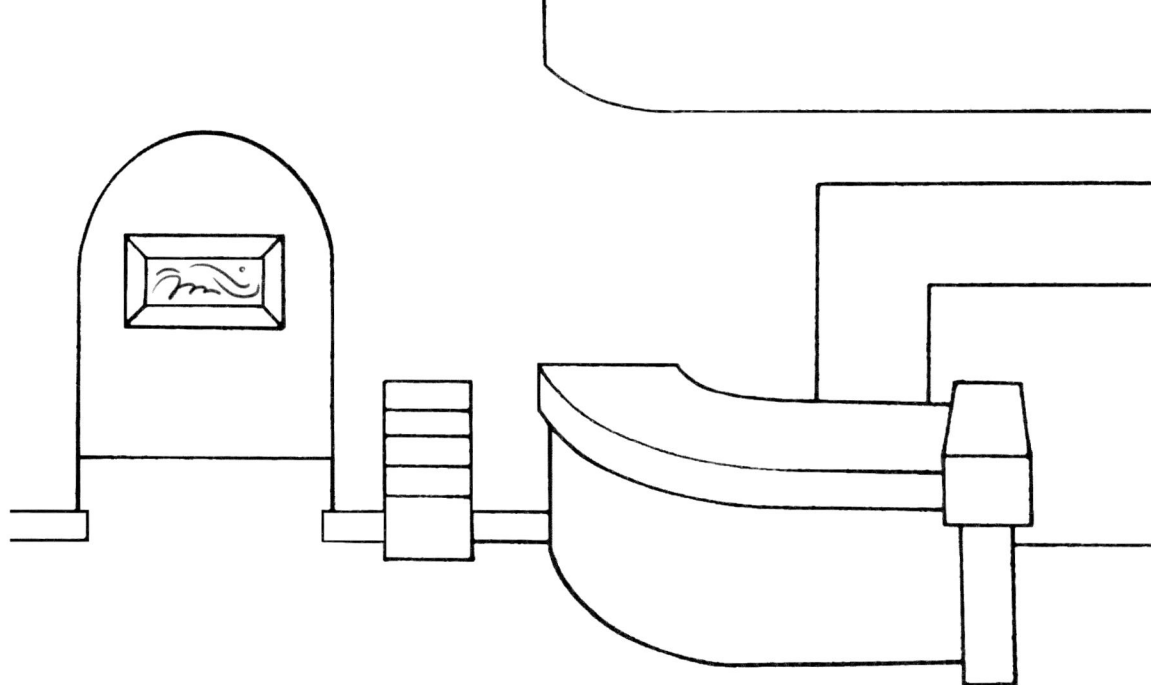

Some preliminary considerations:
- What would be a good *dominant color* for the space? _____

- What sort of *color scheme* (monochromatic, triadic, *et cetera*) would be ideal? _____

- How intense (<u>saturated</u> *versus* <u>dark</u> or <u>light</u>) should the various color(s) (base and accent) be? _____

- Should the palette "lead" the visitor in any way? Where? _____

SCENARIO 2:
The sign-in/checkout business area of a dentist's office.

Situation: Drs. Chris Aiken, Sandy Payne, and Terry Suffern *("Aiken, Payne and Suffern, DDS")* are opening a new practice. They are beset with the normal problems of such an office, such as their patients' worries about cost, fear of physical anguish, and anxiety about waiting. The arch to the left leads to the exquisite torture of the inner sanctum; the rack to the left of the counter contains helpful information about billing practices, dental procedures and religious tracts, which Drs Aiken, Payne and Suffern want people to read. Please color this space for them.

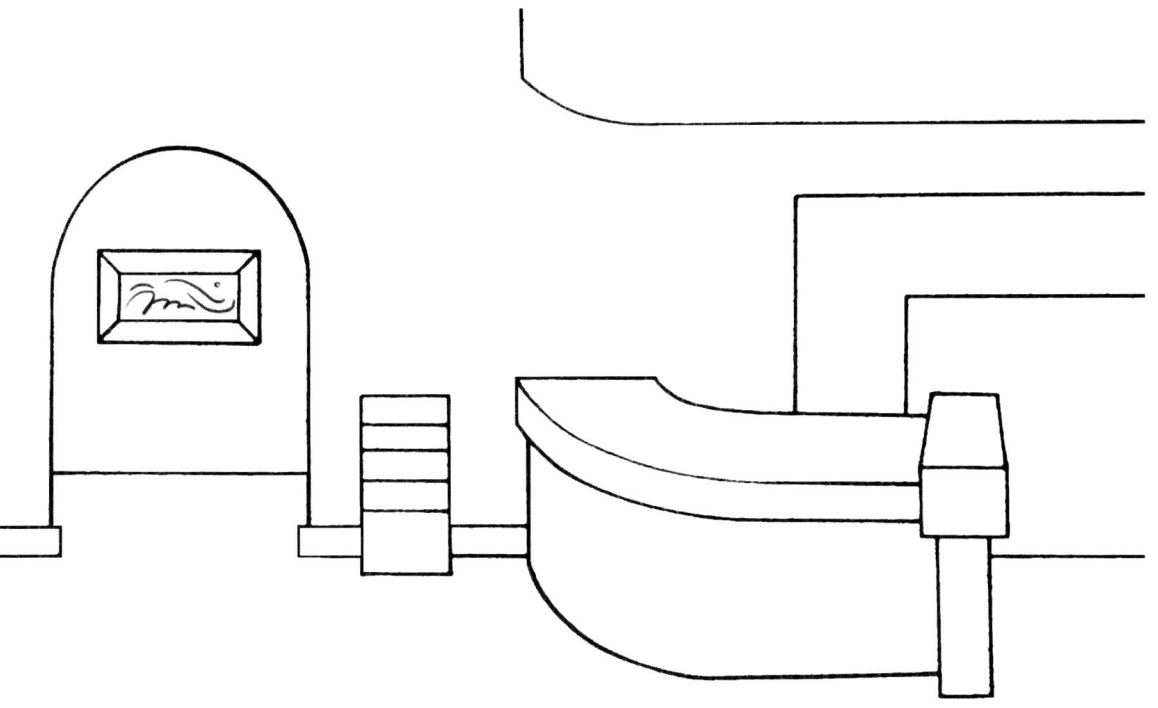

Some preliminary considerations:
- What would be a good *dominant color* for the space? _____

- What *sort* of *color scheme* would work well? _____

- How *intense* should each of the color(s) be? _____

- Should the palette "lead" the visitor in any way? Where? _____

SCENARIO 3:
A retail cash/wrap.

Situation: This is the place where people make their purchases (in tradespeak, the "cash/wrap") at *Castle & Commons,* a huge chain of retail book, CD and magazine stores. Their major competitor, *Infinities,* uses the same marketing strategy, so this area—the last thing the customer sees before leaving—must send a strongly distinctive "message." The arch at left is the exit to the mall in which the store is located; the rack to the left of the counter holds handouts provided by local charities, and the store owners (who do this as a public service) don't care if people pay attention to them or not. Please color this space for them.

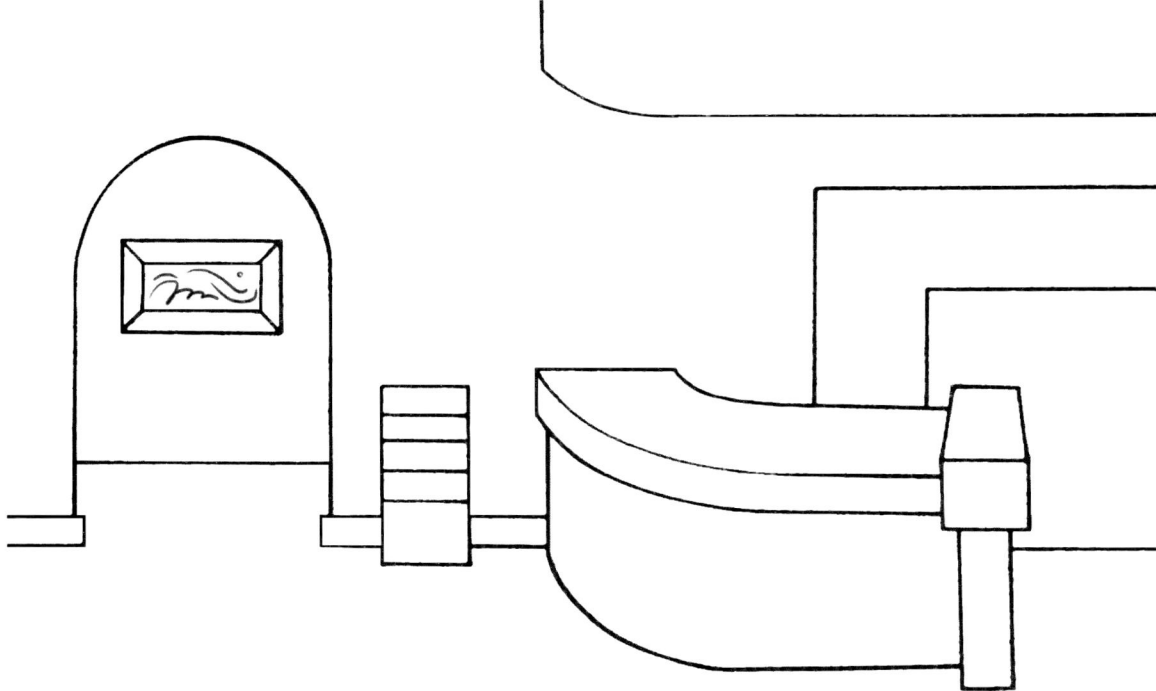

Some preliminary considerations:
- What would be a good *dominant color* for the space? _____
- What *sort* of *color scheme* would work well? _____
- How *intense* should each of the color(s) be? _____
- Should the palette "lead" the visitor in any way? Where? _____

SCENARIO 4:
The information desk in a library.

Situation: Dr. DuBarry Oldburry of the Newberry Library is redesigning the Information and Circulation Desk, which is the principle contact point between the Library staff and their patrons. This will require balancing several concerns, ranging from maintaining the suitable level of silence and respect due such a structure and the staff's desire to appear friendly and welcoming. The arch is the place from which people have come (and to which they are *not* encouraged to return); the rack to the left of the counter contains free periodicals, which the library hopes people will take. Please color this space for them.

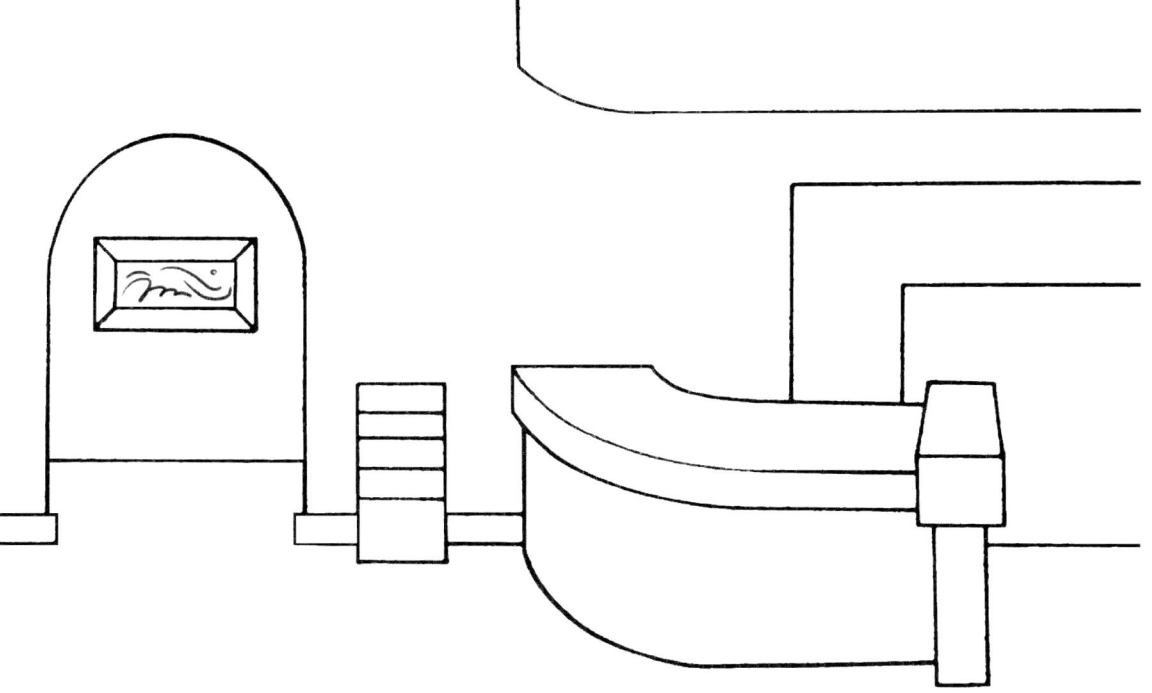

Some preliminary considerations:
- What would be a good *dominant color* for the space? _____
- What *sort* of *color scheme* would work well? _____
- How *intense* should each of the color(s) be? _____
- Should the palette "lead" the visitor in any way? Where? _____

SCENARIO 5:
A trendy, hip bar

Situation: *Carpe Noctem* ("Seize the Night"), a bar catering to the young, the stylish, the elegant, and the beautiful, is planning a great new location in your town. The only thing greater than the flash and dash of its clientele is the cash they spend—and if you have to ask how much their honey-flavored signature drink *("Roo and Rum")* costs, you can't afford it. The arch leads to the toilets; the rack to the left of the counter contains individual waiters' worklists, and the management doesn't want people noticing it. Please color this space for them.

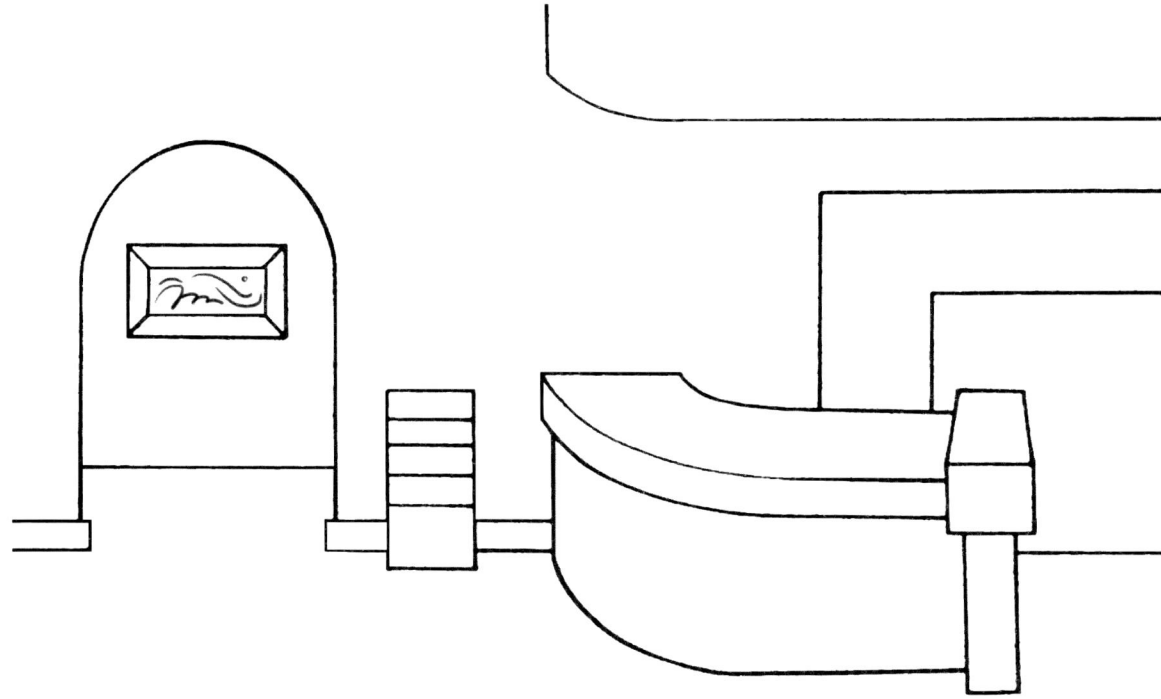

Some preliminary considerations:
- What would be a good *dominant color* for the space? _____
- What *sort* of *color scheme* would work well? _____
- How *intense* should each of the color(s) be? _____
- Should the palette "lead" the visitor in any way? Where? _____

SCENARIO 6:
The "help" desk at an electronics retailer

Situation: *Wol's* is a local stereo, computer and digital camera retailer, competing with the big electronic chains. They hire a few competent people who can stand in a central point in the store and provide useful answers to customers; low-paid drones in the aisles provide easier information. The "Information Center" (shown here) must send several visual messages, such as accessibility, high-tech, and authority. The arch leads to the company's offices (where people shouldn't go); the rack to the left of the counter contains product literature, which the owners very much want to get into customers' hands. Please color this space for them.

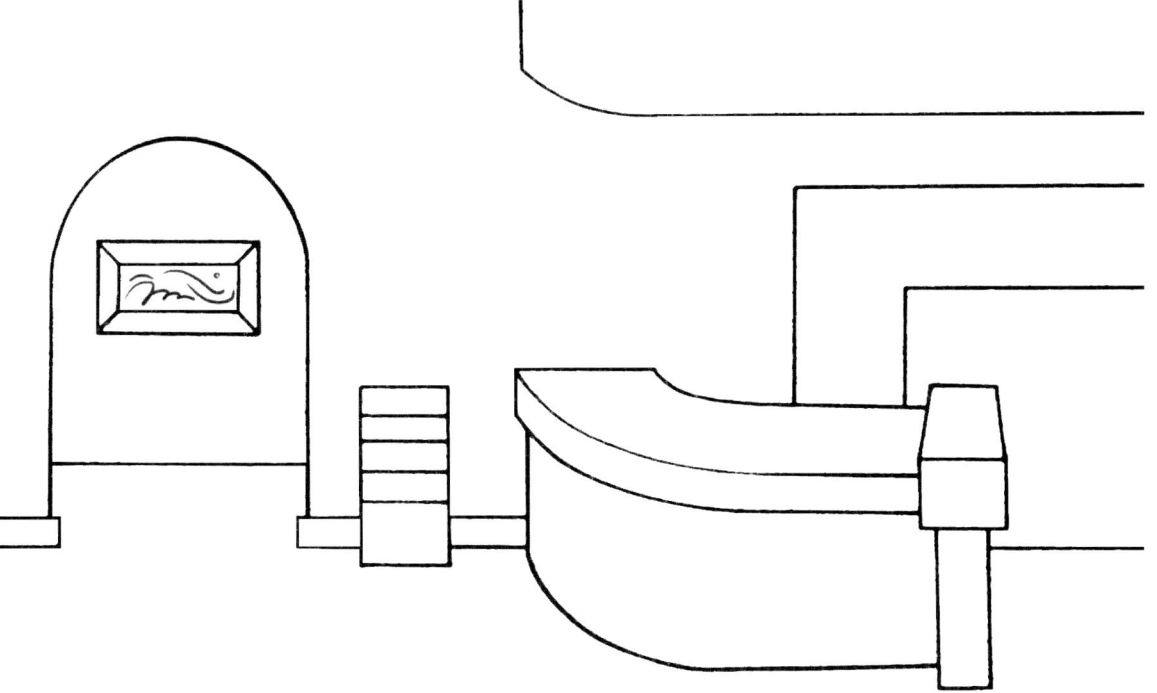

Some preliminary considerations:
- What would be a good *dominant color* for the space? _____
- What *sort* of *color scheme* would work well? _____
- How *intense* should each of the color(s) be? _____
- Should the palette "lead" the visitor in any way? Where? _____

CONCLUSION

Was that fun? This exercise was intended to be an entertaining way for you to practice and internalize the lessons of this little book, encouraging you to go back into the text and make decisions revealing both what you already knew and what you might have learned. Remember, if you want to compare your responses to these scenarios with those of several professionals, please get in touch with the Present Author.

And maybe—just maybe—you have learned so much that you now want to become a decorator yourself. If so, you need to sign up for some courses; in that case—or in *any* case—thanks for reading this book, and best wishes in all you do hereafter!

Gerry Poster

About the Author

Gerry Poster (Gerbrand Poster III), has been an author and trainer for over 30 years. He specializes in communications, problem-solving, persuasion and other forms of selling, team-building, continuous improvement, and diversity cooperation. He has provided training, merchandising, and manufacturing support to the carpet industry for almost 30 years; he began consulting with Masland's sister companies in 1992, and joined the Dixie Group family in 1995.

Gerry graduated from the University of the South (Sewanee) and Rice University. He served as an officer in the US Navy, and taught at the Naval Academy (Annapolis) and Clemson University before directing his energies to corporate training. He has received subsequent certifications from groups such as Phil Crosby Associates, Learning International, the Forum Group, and similar organizations. He has designed many training programs for individual companies as diverse as optical retailers and auto-industry suppliers.

Gerry prescribes a comprehensive approach to organizational management and development, which is described in his books such as *Trade Secrets: How Successful Leaders Get the Job Done Right the First Time* (about leading continuous improvement), *Natural Feelings, Unnatural Acts (A Professional's Guide to Effective Persuasive Communications)*, *MAST (Masland Applied Sales Training)*, *QP³: Quality People, Quality Processes, Quality Products* (driving continuous improvement into the work force), *The PIG Pack* and *The Bat Book* (hands-on problem-solving tools), *Shibboleths and Shorthand* (an introduction to interior design and architecture), *The Carpet and Rug Handbook,* and *Cat Herding for Fun and Profit*. Masland's clients have direct access to Gerry's help from his offices in South Carolina.

"Colors fade, temples crumple, empires fall, but wise words endure."
—Edward Thorndike